The Creator Connection

MW01688651

Healing Series—#1

The Creator Connection

Your Spiritual Guidebook

Silver Eagle

Writers Club Press
San Jose New York Lincoln Shanghai

The Creator Connection
Your Spiritual Guidebook

All Rights Reserved © 2001 by Silver Eagle

No part of this book may be reproduced or transmitted in any form or by any means, graphic, electronic, or mechanical, including photocopying, recording, taping, or by any information storage retrieval system, without the permission in writing from the publisher.

Writers Club Press
an imprint of iUniverse.com, Inc.

For information address:
iUniverse.com, Inc.
5220 S 16th, Ste. 200
Lincoln, NE 68512
www.iuniverse.com

ISBN: 0-595-18469-3

Printed in the United States of America

For all those who dream and have dreamed of another way,

for those who are not perfect and are beginning to wonder,

for those who have lived so long with the sword they've forgotten love.

May the path I've walked help you in yours.

Remember that the demons we face are not all outside of us.

"The unexamined life is not worth living."

Socrates

Contents

Foreword

I have spent many a rainy afternoon watching the drops slip quietly down the window pane and wondering… I wondered where the rain came from, where it was going, how many others' lives would it touch on its journey through this world and would I somehow be a part of that by the witnessing of one tiny sparkling drop of dew. I would imagine that it came from the Far East where the language of life would be much different from mine. I imagined that through its travels it had swirled in the oceans of the earth and perhaps splashed off the back of a dolphin before evaporating, condensing and finally landing on the sill of my window to the world. Perhaps on another day, it had fallen on the window of another girl just like me, wondering where her drop came from and where it was going. I imagined the grass whose thirst would be slackened by the chance meeting I'd had with mother nature. Or would it really matter at all that I was there at that time to see that particular drop form and continue on its way? I would follow it deep into the ground as it was absorbed into the thirsty soil. There I envisioned a flower in the soil drawing up the precious life fluid until it bloomed out of sheer joy.

As we are all different from one in other, I was different from most. This was only one of my pondering hobbies that prepared me for a life I would contemplate and question the nature of forever, or until Creator gets tired of my questions. The musings of youth gave way to the 'realities' of growing up and the challenges that come with peer pressure. Bad enough to be different inside, but I was disabled as well, wearing leg braces until sixth grade. Main streaming in the public schools was still new at the time and kids, faced with uncertainty and fear can be very cruel. I learned early that to be different was not only considered wrong but dangerous. I spent the majority of my school years either unwilling punching bag of the bully of the week or the fastest pigeon-toed runner in my school.

My parents were divided on their advice to me about how to handle the situations. My mother was a turn the other cheek advocate so, most of the time, I'd get that one kicked too. My father told me to fight back but I really didn't want to hurt anyone else. I knew what it felt like. My mother said it was because they didn't understand me, or at least that's what I heard in my child mind. So I thought, if they understood me, understood that they hurt me on the inside and the outside, maybe they would stop. Needless to say, that didn't work but it did set the tone for my life. From that day on I would work to understand others whether it helped or not. I found that while it didn't win me brownie points when push came to shove, it did help me to divert them and avoid punishment together if I understood them.

So from that dubious beginning I became a people pleaser and conformist. It was easier to just try to fit in than anything else but I was abysmal at that. I'm not a very convincing liar and soon was labeled quite prominently an outcast. So I reevaluated my approach. I reasoned that if I understood them and it still didn't work, maybe I needed to explain myself to them. If they knew me better, maybe then they'd like me. I was in junior high around that time. It turned into a highly useful skill in the end but didn't produce the results I'd hoped. In understanding what I did of myself and them, there was very little to build anything in hopes of friendships. Consequently, I had a very close small circle of friends.

Entering High school I'd just about given up on any sort of understanding except from the few close friends I had. We had our own little group of 'outcasts.' Then came the Drama Club and through some twist of fate that perhaps only the God of puberty understands, the little group I shared was very good at. Soon, everyone wanted to be with us and we were popular. To be out was to be 'in.' For once in my life, the cool kids actually wanted to copy me. I wasn't a cool kid but I was in. I had respect so long as they wanted something from me. I soon grew tired of the trap that comes with popularity. The whole time, all I'd wanted was acceptance and I still didn't have that. It would be 20 years before I even knew what that was and how to have it.

I'm sure my story isn't unique. Most people in their youth have felt unaccepted by someone whose opinion they respected. Most have tried in the same ways I did to get it and have failed as well. We are a nation of people pleasers trying to kiss up to the bullies just to eek out a passable existence when all we really want is someone to understand and share with us our expressions of hope and life. From that understanding, we know we have somewhere to belong, somewhere safe from careless judgments, somewhere to simply be.

I've learned through my life that acceptance has to come from within to mean anything at all. In many case that's easier said than done but you cannot be whole until you do. What you accept, you take in and make a part of you and your understanding. It is the single largest factor in decision making skills and coping mechanisms. The power of choice itself is limited by what we will and will not accept or take in. And the need for acceptance is greatest way we manipulate and destroy each other. If you can learn to accept yourself, you gain immunity to the strains and struggles of everyday life. For some it's as simple as changing a thought but for others like me, life has done too much to you. You can't just turn it off. For those like me, you must understand in order to accept. That's what this book is about.

I'm not a doctor, though I've studied on my own out of pure delight in curiosity. I'm not a psychiatrist, though I have been to a few in my day. I'm not a physicist but have taken up particle physics and theoretical physics as a hobby. I would have fit right in with Pythagoras and his crowd with one difference, I want to understand and explore not just know. Knowing is secondary to me. I never went to college. I speak from the authority of my own experiences and what they meant to me and that's all. What I *have* done is explore the melting sunset, knowing that it's rising somewhere else far away from me. I've marveled at the pallet of colors that dance off the atmospheric vapors simply sighed at the beauty of it all. I've traveled and known people from all over the world and know for a fact what my mom would colorfully explain to me as a child, "They all put their pants on the same way, one leg at a time." Ideas may be different, views change, bitter enemies become fast friends, but the human heart hasn't changed much over the millennia. Forever seeking, forever hoping, it beats to the rhythm of our collective steps unsure of where it's taking us but certain it must go nonetheless.

So today, I'll watch the rain once again and reflect. I haven't changed at all, I'm afraid. Sure, I know now that it's simply H2O molecules that have bonded through electrical means and gotten too heavy. Gravity tugged the water into a drop that followed its Newtonian sensibilities and landed on the pane of melted sand and other chemicals we call glass. I know now where it's going, how it got there, what it'll do and what it means to me to be a part of it all. But I still don't understand why and I don't think I really want to. I just want to *be* in the wonder of it all.

Acknowledgements

Special Thanks:

Reverend Sherry Mullins for her encouragement and spiritual guidance. She doesn't even know what she did for me.

Jackie Harper, for listening to me go on and on about the publishing process.

To the gang in Florida—they know who they are.

To my kids for teaching me to grow up.

To my husband who listened to me go on for hours and hours about what I was thinking no matter what time it was.

And last but not least, my Mom and Dad.
They've always been there for me even when I didn't know it.

Introduction

This book is intended to be used as a workbook. As such, it contains several pages at the back of the chapters in which to journal your experiences as you go. It is, and has been, my small crusade that experience is the best and most accurate teacher when it comes to individual trials. I designed this book to lead you to your own experiences through learning about yourself. To this end, writing is an excellent way of preserving thoughts and feelings to review when your eyes are clearer and hindsight is most useful. I realize that many people don't want to 'work'. They would rather take a pill, learn a catch phrase, or find someone to make it all better for them. But for those of us brave enough to own ourselves and maybe bring a few others with us, this is an effective tool. What you learn here and gain for yourself, you gain for others in all the lives you will touch during your lifetime. To know the way and be able to share it is a gift.

This book is *not* intended to take the place of advice given by a qualified physician, care giver, or other professional.

One more thing… Use what you need from these words and leave the rest behind. It is my greatest hope that you find many things in here that apply in your life and your path. But all ways are not for everyone. Sometimes we are only meant to cross one in others paths —not walk together.

Check It Out

http://thecreatorconnection.tripod.com/1.html for updates on the authors new books, readers forum, and e-zine! Also check site for information and a sample recording of her upcoming music CD *Shadows*—due out January 2002.

Write the author at—**creatorconnection@hotmail.com**

Chapter One

Questions

First Words

The first chapter is devoted to laying groundwork for a common understanding of basic ingredients when interpreting the human condition. These snatches and bits of psyche are common to most who live and wonder what it's all about. This chapter will show you the foundation of tools you'll need to begin the journey toward healing yourself.

Material Preparation: Envelope
Open, inquisitive mind
Honesty

Assignment

Make some time during the day where you won't be disturbed. Sit comfortably in front of a mirror. Have a pen and pad of paper handy or use the journal space provided at the end of this chapter. (Make certain it's a pen. It's harder to change.) Begin with these questions.

Physical:
1) What do my eyes see?
2) What do I want to change?
3) What am I willing to change?
4) What am I willing to accept?
5) What am I afraid of?

Mental:
1) What do I think I know?
2) What do I want to know but don't?
3) What am I afraid to know?
4) What am I afraid to accept?

Emotional:
1) What do I feel about myself?
2) What am I afraid to feel?
3) What have I become for everyone else?
4) What have I become for myself?

Do not add hows and whys to this list or you will confuse yourself. Stick to the whats. You must see all the whats clearly or nothing else will make sense. Answer them as completely and honestly as you can. If you're good at deception, then you know when you're doing it. If you are not, then you are not inclined to lie to yourself anyway. Either way, there's no reason you have to cheat yourself. Do not stop until you answer all of them. Write even if it doesn't make sense. That reasoning helped me through the roughest times.

When you've finished answering the questions just sit observing yourself for a while with one question in mind: Who am I? Allow yourself to ponder the question but do not answer it yet. There are times the journey is more important than the destination and this is one. You're about to take a hell of a journey! When you are finished, place what you wrote in an envelope in a special place or leave it in the book. We'll be using it in an exercise at the end of the book.

Let's bake a cake. By the time we are done, the cake will be you. Before anything, we need a container. I assume everyone who is reading this has a body and it's equipped with the basics or optional alternatives. Every soul needs somewhere to live after all. Next, before we even start, we need to be sure you have all the ingredients. It just wouldn't work to bake a chocolate cake only to find we didn't have chocolate. Remember, there's no substitute for the real thing.

Ingredients for Healing

You can lead a horse to water. You can show the horse there's nothing to be afraid of by swimming in the water. You can cup your hand and drizzle some on his snout to prove it won't harm him. You can physically grab him and put him in the water…but you will only succeed in drowning him. The only thing the same about all of us is that we are all different. We move to diverse, and sometimes opposing rhythms and ideas. Respect for that in others and yourself is essential to healing. Without it, you become arrogant and controlling, lost in your fears. With it, you become compassionate, understanding, and patient. Respect is a process of placing value on differences. We are each a world unto ourselves living within a universe with a balance uniquely it's own. We must care for our 'world' as best we can.

Will

We've all met the three-time loser. You know, the one who despite every observable condition to the contrary and no matter how hard they try, reality craps on them anyway. It never seems their fault. They see themselves as victims and so do others. They just seem to have bad luck. People like that are victims, not of others or the universe but of themselves and misapplied will. It's hard work to remain negative in a world where multiple polarity exists. It's an indication that their will is strong—just applied against them. Because of this, they are closed to learning. You cannot teach yourself or anyone else something they are unwilling to learn. This is both the blessing and curse of freedom of our will. There must be some part inside that consents or there will be no lasting or meaningful results.

Willingness opens a door for the exchange of energy from one place to another. Each of us was born with the ability to act—literally, as we received a body for that. When we act, our personal energy goes forward from us into that action and in turn interacts with the energies of this reality. The energy comes back to us as experience. Willingness engages us on a conscious level in this energy exchange.

Without willingness, the cycle of exchange is lopsided. You aren't open so there is little or no flow. However, this universe was in motion long before you. This reality is built for the purpose of exchange. When you use your will to stop it instead of participate in it, the energy has to go somewhere so it bounces around you seeking exchange. You may feel constantly under attack, reactive, and stressed. Relationships fall into dependence and disrepair. You will be unable to stick to anything you begin and the cycle of negativity goes on and on. Like a snowball rolling downhill, once your will weakens, it will stay that way until you change it. To truly heal yourself, you must be willing to see a weakness, confront it, and understand it.

Determination

This is not the type of swashbuckling determination that keeps you in hopeless battles with your ego but the type that keeps your spirit going, no matter what you find. The only one who will ever truly give up on you is you. When the going gets tough, you just keep on because your desire to be whole is greater than whatever you may find in your 'flaws.' Your desire to take back power in your life transcends any negativity you may stumble on. It's that simple. To say it in a catchy proactive phrase—fall down six times, get up seven.

Just as your body has arms and legs, every spirit has these abilities that enable them to effectively navigate the physical, mental and emotional aspects of their life. The spiritual aspect comes into focus when you uncover a fundamental truth common to all the aspects. Now that you have the ingredients, you need the tools that will combine them effectively into experience.

Tools of Transformation

Choice is the active application of your will; one of the most versatile and powerful tools to that there is. There are only two choices you will ever make in your life, action and non action. Within action there are three choices: positive, negative, and neutral. Non action is the choice not to choose. It is a fundamental, inescapable truth of existence here. The ability to choose guarantees that each individual will determine their own path in life.

There are two basic types of choice. There's situational choice—What are you going to do? This is normally preceded by an event; your car breaks down. Since effect always follows cause, what are you going to do? (The ability to adapt) I call a mechanic, simple, smooth and effective. Out of myriad choices you picked one and initiated it. Goody for you.

The other type of choice is personal choice. This is where most people get stuck because they don't understand it. Personal choice is how this event will affect you on the mental and emotional levels. People are unaware of this choice because they've learned to be reactionary. Here is an example of personal choice. I am upset so I kick and scream at the car.

Personal choice is subject to the same cause and effect laws as situational choice but carries a heavier penalty than physical laws do. I kick the car—stub my toe. I scream at the car—lose my voice. Even if neither of those happens, if you let events such as these get to you then they control your outlook for the rest of the day. This is how the negative viewpoint gets started. If you can learn how to understand your reactions and change them, you can change your life. The way you use choice changes and starts a chain reaction that transforms your life.

To begin to build awareness of the choices you make you must start with First Choice, to live. Bad things happen. That's reality. If that's true, than how can choice be a power in your life at all? First choice for all of us is to live. If it were not, you wouldn't be here now. A traumatic event happens and leaves you picking up the pieces of your life; you choose to live. Build your awareness around that acceptance. I choose to live. Too many take for granted that they breathe and are alive. Life may be a gift but there is a powerful realization in knowing that you choose to be alive. You are participating in a grand adventure full of danger and pleasure. Even if all you do is sit in front of the TV, you are alive. Not by some accident, not just by gift but because you choose to be.

The Can'ts of Life

My mother is from the old country. She used to tell me that can't-never-did-do-nothing and she was right. Most of the time people say the word can't, they are really saying won't, which is a function of will and choice. The true can'ts of life fall within the realm of things beyond our power of choice such as limitations set in place by the physical implications of living. Example: I can't walk. I have no legs. That's a legitimate can't. When you use can't, it should be a reflection of inability, not unwillingness. Therefore, I can't make up my mind is an inaccurate statement. You certainly can make up your mind. You have the capability. You simply do not want to make only one choice or you aren't fond of any of the choices available. Every time you misuse the word can't, you place a limitation on your ability to change your life. Just change the viewpoint. It sounds simple but I guarantee it's the hardest thing to do. But then, what things truly worthwhile aren't?

Patience

Besides being the proverbial virtue, patience is one of the most useful tools to have in your arsenal. First you must learn to recognize change itself. Winter becomes spring; spring becomes summer; summer becomes fall and in turn becomes winter again. Half of the reason that a situation becomes intolerable is that you don't see it changing from one state to another. In the minds eye, what is really perceived is no improvement from the previous state. That gives the illusion that the situation is stagnant, makes us want to force movement of any kind.

Through choice, we direct the energy behind that movement. Change, for better or worse is still change and if you train the mind to focus on the change rather than the judgments of that change, the frustrations of life and situations become manageable, tolerable. The good news is that no thing lasts forever. That's also the bad news.

Change itself is more of an acceptance than an achievement. For this reason, it is difficult to master. How do you grasp something that is constantly in motion? It is in effect, an infinite. I was determined though. I figured that nothing changes faster than the weather where I was at. I sat for hours watching the clouds go by to even get the merest inkling of the concept. It is through the acceptance that you understand, even if you can't pin it down in words. Patience is how we express the speed of change, how the infinite moves through the finite. Once you realize and accept it, you seek out that recognition to use as a coping skill. You learn to look for the advantages of change as well as the disadvantages to aid you in the choices you make.

Observation

This is the ability to maintain a neutral viewpoint and discern possible options in a situation. The hardest part of this skill is the neutrality required to effectively observe. Sometimes this is interpreted as a scientific, logical, and unemotional viewpoint however, that is a misinterpretation. Neutrality is a pivot in the forces of positive and negative, and more to the point, a power that exists not exclusive of positive and negative but rather inclusive of both. Here is where another element of observation becomes important, the need for balance. Balance is not a resting or stationary quality but rather a constant movement of those forces. Stand on one foot and you'll see what I mean. Sometimes it will tilt farther one way sometimes the other but the result of the struggle will be balance between the two, so long as you keep in motion. Accurate balance will help you achieve neutrality once you become used to it.

So here's how the tools work together: Balance supports neutrality. Neutrality supports observation. Observation supports patience. Patience supports choice. Choice transforms your life. All the tools and ingredients to your cake intertwine and connect in ways that are unique to you and at the same time, basic to all of us. Sort of a basic recipe for a human as if when the human condition was created, though varying in amounts, intensity, shades, and qualities, all humans have these ingredients in some form.

Realizing First Choice

To realize something is to make real by the understanding of it. To truly understand something you must first experience it. Experience brings concepts, thoughts, and visions from the subconscious into the conscious where they become physical manifestations. If you know something—it is just knowledge/ information. However, if you've experienced something, you'll understand the substance of that information, how it fits, why it fits and how to apply it. For example: you can make a cake; acquire the ingredients, measure them, balance them, mix them, bake them and still you don't really know a cake until you taste it. You simply know about it. There is a world of difference. When you chew, roll it on your tongue, savor the taste, feel it with every fiber of awareness, digest it and apply it to yourself and make it a part of you—only then you can say you know it; you understand it. That's when you realize it. That's the passion of life.

Exercise

Step one—Close your eyes. Place your feet flat on the floor and begin to breathe in through the nose, out through the mouth. Picture the distractions of the day as wax figures that melt into nothingness with every exhalation until your mind is free. Enjoy this state for a few moments before continuing.

Step two—Become aware of the air expanding within your body and feel it leave in the exhale. With every breath reach deeper into yourself. Allow yourself to feel the active choice you make in living by the simple act of breathing. Every breath is an agreement to continue breathing, continue living. Begin to experience it in each cell of your body.

Step three—Allow it to consciously fill every emotion, every fiber, every muscle, every bone. Feel it pulsate as it circulates around your body bringing with it an infusion of warm energy.

Step four—Consciously draw energy in with each breath through the nose, hold for a moment and release through the mouth. Continue this exercise until you feel you are finished. Usually, the energy will begin to recede on its own when you have reached a tolerable level. Do not be surprised if it takes a while for it to dissipate. Many people are virtually starved energy-wise.

Step five—Become consciously aware that this energy is the river of your living spirit connected to that which sustains and nurtures it.

This should be practiced ideally, three times a day. Minimum—two times, morning and night while working with this book.

Step six—Write about your experiences in the space provided.

Last Words

This realization is a moment with you and your Creator and is personal and unique to everyone. By exercising your choice to live you become a partner with your Creator in your life. That realization becomes the source of your strength and is something no one can ever take away from you. In that moment, you begin your journey, not mine, not the ministers, not your friends but yours. This is your first conscious moment of self.

Write about your experiences. These words of reflection are invaluable to being able to understand yourself through your experiences, not because of them.

Journal Space

Chapter Two

The Basics

First Words

Chapter Two is designed to show you how you and your environment are connected and interact with one in other. In this chapter you identify fundamental landmarks of the self, both within and without, to strengthen the steps along your journey.

Material Preparation:	Two days (an uninterrupted mealtime) Two favorite meals (one for each day) Desire to grow

Challenge: There are those who do not believe in a Creator. This is a weak viewpoint. Disprove the existence of a Creator.

There are those who believe without question in a Creator. This is also a weak viewpoint. Prove that the other ones are wrong.

Few dispute the idea that there is something greater than any of us, they only fight over what to call it. That's why I have chosen the word Creator. Whether you see a man with a white beard on top of a mountain or the mysterious reason why cells divide, creation is within everything and everyone. This is one of the things that I define as basic—a fundamental truth manifesting through all levels of thought and all states of being.

What is understood about physical reality breaks down on the subatomic level. Study of emotional awareness is helpful but only goes so far. Whether you study particle physics, cosmology, or religion eventually, you run out of answers and have to say, 'I don't know.' That is the moment of awareness within which you experience a Creator. In the moment you can admit you don't know but you are willing to begin; you open to the infinite resources and possibilities of creation. It is what is known in Tao as unlearning what you have learned.

Origin

Everything is. This is a good place, if ambiguous, to start. Everything from here becomes how we define, not only the world but ourselves in relation to it. Because everything is, everything can be used to help or harm. That's where choice and intent become involved.

Base of Basic Growth

Every living thing grows; every nonliving thing accumulates. Without this basic truth there would be no movement and no motivation to move. Growth is the basic movement of life; the flow of a great river we are all a part of. It is the one thing that all life has in common. Every day you are constantly adding to yourself on all levels of awareness, not accumulating but actually adding. Websters defines adding as causing an increase or joining one with another so there will be more. Whether it's positive or negative is entirely up to you depending on what level you are dealing with, but life is always evolving forward no matter what it's disguise in the moment. By the minute, by the second, by the day you are always more than what you were. It guarantees the momentum of change and that choice will always be a dominate force for directing your life.

Connections

The simplicity of the concept is that everything and everyone are connected, including you. Think about what that means. As a pebble introduced into water creates a ripple, everything you are and do affect everything else. Choices are like pebbles tossed into the river of your life. Where you place them determines where and how the river flows. Conversely, if you chose not to place a pebble, the river will continue to flow in the same manner, same crap, different day.

Why should you bother to work at understanding it at all? Why not choose to accept all of these as life's mysteries and go from there? You can, but for me acceptance without exploration has never been enough. I have found that each person has to determine those answers for themselves to have a solid foundation when things get tough. Effective exploration of those two questions will tell you more about yourself than I ever could. I ask myself these constantly. Every time I find what looks like an answer it's just the next question in disguise so in reality, I have both at the same time. I feel emptiness and satisfaction at the same time. I experience my knowledge and ignorance at the same time. I see where I've been and where I'm going because I know where I am. That's when I know I've accomplished something real. That's when I experience myself and, within that I experience a connection with Creator. Everyone whom I've taken through this process has experienced the same basic steps, though, the way they went about them varied because their answers were different from mine. My 'proof' of these connections came from observing the processes of life. There's truth to the words, "There are many paths but only one journey."

Consider: Everything is composed of atoms. Even material from outer space displays the same blueprints of atomic development that can be found here in both living and nonliving things. The fundamentals of atomic structure have variety but the basics never change. A defiant electron here creates a new element there and we have a fish instead of a cow but the basic ingredients never change they vary. Basically there are protons, neutrons, electrons, a nucleus and a few other stray leptons and such. Every atom has these traits without fail. You never find an atom without a nucleus but the rest of the content will be different according to what you're studying.

Consider: The human body is composed of cells; they divide and multiply, create more cells just like themselves and somehow diversify according to a preprogrammed map, but the basics never change—they simply vary. Atoms gather—living cells divide to create more of themselves. Both processes are similar and yet dependent on one in other. No atoms—no cells.

Consider: Countless universes out there—you are a part of one. (Maybe more if you lived through the sixties.) At least 28 local galaxies in this universe—you are a part of the Milky Way. About a hundred billion possible solar systems in this galaxy—you are in one. Nine planets in this solar system (though the debate about that continues)—you are on Earth. Seven continents on this planet—you are on one. Depending on which continent, there are several states—you are in one. Several cities in this state—you are in one. Several neighborhoods in this city—you are in one. Several blocks in the neighborhood—you are on one. Several homes on the block—you are in one. Several rooms in the house—you are in one. Several pieces of furniture in the room—you are on one. It is the same pattern of connections from the other direction.

Consider music: Composed of simple notes lead by rhythm, not unlike the cells of the body driven by the rhythm of your breathing.

Notes in themselves are simple tone sounded for a specific length of time. Even drums are tuned to a distinctive note. A group of like notes are considered a key. A group of like cells are called an organ; a group of like atoms, an element. A solar system is a family of planets in a like orbit. Even if you argue that all of this is simply case of how we classify the world around us then you have to ask yourself why would it be classified that way if a pattern of connections didn't exist.

All these examples illustrate the process of creation in action, where everything and everyone are connected. Every living person has cells that are in constant motion, constantly exchanging, multiplying and dying. Think about that next time you're at a party. Atoms are in constant motion within those cells and every other material thing, on this world and others. Even light particles are constantly moving, always keeping the basics but varying everything else to suit the needs or conditions of the moment.

If this much is true, if on the ground floor of development it's all the same, then everything is truly connected in a great web of life. Chief Seattle expressed it best, "What we do to the web, we do to ourselves." What goes around eventually comes around. One thing leads to another. You tell two friends and they tell two friends and so on and so on and so on… This is also the internal pattern of how we grow and can heal. If you can grasp the design apart from yourself then it's a short hop, skip and jump to understanding it within yourself. You become closer to Creator by understanding what has been created, namely yourself.

Going Within

Levels of Thought:

Thought is the beginning and continuance of everything within the self, the seed of Creator and infinity. Webster defines thought as a process or power. The movement of thought becomes the energy we use to live much as a ripple in the water creates waves at the shore as it expands. Because everything living grows, thoughts gain momentum and energy as they expand proportionally to the level they're manifest on.

You have four basic levels but we'll only deal with three for now: physical, emotional, and mental. Within this system there are connections—places where they intersect.

On the Physical level
Physical/Physical
Physical/Emotional
Physical/Mental

On the Emotional level
Emotional/Physical
Emotional/Emotional
Emotional/Mental

On the Mental level
Mental/Physical
Mental/Emotional
Mental/Mental

Now, though it can be argued that the origin of all these areas may or may not be based in thought (as in the thought of the Creator), it is widely accepted that thought influences all of these aspects of the self with significant impacts on the health and well-being of the entire organism. Just as the nervous system gives electrical impulses places to go, these connections give your thoughts places to go. Inside each of these levels are webs within webs looping around themselves and connecting with every aspect of your being providing a basic framework for communication within the system.

Perspective

This is where and how you find yourself in relation to the 'is' and Creator. Imagine: A star reaches the 'end' of its life and, with a final burst of energy, it explodes. Pieces of it go shooting off into the void of space, some entering other gravitational fields to become moons, some becoming comets, some asteroids... Now, imagine that you are a piece of that star facing what's left of where you thought of as home. How you view it will be drastically different from how the piece that became the moon views it because you are in different places, even different times when you get right down to it. You were there and now you're here. Perspective provides definition and identity to form a foundation for exploration of thought. Throughout the growth process your perspective changes and you find new experiences to draw from. This is transformation on the very basic of levels. As with energy in physics, thoughts are never extinguished but rather, transformed from one state to another.

Perspective can also be where you find yourself in relation to your fears. This is not such a good thing. As rose-colored glasses present to you a world with only one color, perceiving through your fears gives you nothing but those fears in their mirrored forms. When you perceive through fear, you become reactive to those around you and to the world. Your thoughts dwell on what could happen instead of what is happening. 'What if's' dominate your thoughts and become paralyzing to choice. This causes fear to become the primary identity thought pattern you become accustomed to. How do you fix that? Keep reading. Do the work. Relearn the pattern.

Internal basics

Within the self, there are three forces that affect thought. These forces cause thought to curve and loop much as a magnet draws metal filings to one area or another, positive (that which adds), negative (that which subtracts) and the balance of the two. In every choice you make there are all three aspects to explore. If you succumb to one or two without acknowledging all of them, you become unbalanced. An imbalance creates a void or chink in the armor that may be exploited by the other forces. A table cannot stand without at least three legs to support it. As in navigation, you need two reference points to find the third. Combining the forces of thought provide you with a broader reference for potentials as well as maintaining balance.

Communication

Within your body right now, cells are exchanging carbon for oxygen; atoms are swapping one electron for two others, hormones are helping various vitamins to connect with each other and build new compounds, the basic chemical content of the bagel you ate this morning is being broken into proteins and distributed all over your body. Right now!

Your entire body depends upon communication on every level. The interpretation is a matter of perspective. Communication begins with the interaction of thoughts with each other and expands into the physical worlds from there. Hundreds of electrical impulses flood the motor pathways of your nervous system just to pick up a cup of coffee. One little uppity neuron can mean that you drop it instead of raising it to your lips. One irritated dendrite on the surface of the skin causes an annoying itch that troubles you for the entire day. It is truly mind boggling. The loops get even more complex the further out the ripples expand. This exchanging creates what we call communication.

There are four ways to exercise communication of thought. The first is through simple passing of information. I tell you something and then you tell me something. Now we both have information we didn't have before. For many people this is the only form of communication they understand. It's also the safest. There is no responsibility for mutual understanding in this form save for the merest of facts. It keeps people at a distance and leaves much open to interpretation. Example: How are you today? This phrase is my personal pet peeve. If anyone asks me this they'd better be prepared to sit and listen to exactly how I am. Most of the social forms of communication are examples of this. How many people do you talk to a day that say this but don't really care about it? On a social level, everyone has agreed that this is an appropriate acknowledgment of existence and recognition.

Sometimes however, it's an invitation to the second exercise of communication. This level involves mutual responsibility for understanding by sharing the communication. This is accomplished by personal comments instead of social ones. Example: "How are you today?" "I'm having a lousy day." Since everyone has had one of those, you've found common ground for discussion without creating too much responsibility for the other person. Their response will determine whether the conversation goes any further. I have developed some unusual and rare friendships by venturing into the personal conversations instead of the social ones. Course I've been viewed as a nut too. The difference between the first and second is the level of personal commitment to sharing. In the first example, you are required only to witness what the other person said and even that is optional these days. In the second example, you are required to give a bit of yourself.

The third exercise of communication involves a greater personal commitment. This is one of the two levels that healing occurs. On this level you must exchange communication by sharing and receiving. This requires an investment of time and energy in maintaining a healthy transfer of understanding between people. Example: "How are you?" "I've had a lousy day." "So did I." "What happened to you?" Communication proceeds from there so long as both parties are listening and sharing. They may not be able to resolve what happened during the day but they can share it and the sharing itself heals. A drop of poison on the tongue kills. A drop of poison in the ocean doesn't.

The fourth exercise of communication is silence. In the wisdom of Tao, it's described as the cessation of competition. It may seem like a huge leap from silence to competition but it's not. To understand the connection you must first ask, 'What is considered competition?'

Websters dictionary defines competition as a contest between groups or individuals. Generally, this is the social perception but it is severely lacking in substance. When one team is against the other, they are competing. Competing for what? Therein lies the real definition of competition.

Competition happens when one or more elements are against each other and a value is determined. This is a very significant point to make. When one is against another, it is to establish value and nothing else. Generally, the stronger is assigned the value of winning and the relative value of 'good.' The weaker is robbed of its value and judgment is born.

So what is value? Value is where attention is concentrated. 'To the victor go the spoils.' Where attention is concentrated, so is energy. This is what I consider to be at the heart of all communication. Underneath all the caring, love, progress, etc., communication, in its many forms, is how energy is passed, transformed, and processed from one source to another. This is at the center of the drive for competition. The winner gets the lions' share of energy from the value assigned to them.

All verbal communication is a way to stake your territory; let others know where you stand for a variety of reasons and rationalizations. All communication is geared for response so the other persons can either dispute or validate your position and thereby your worth. This is the value stage and the place where competition is born.

If you were to translate this from psychological terms to energy exchange, this is the tug of war between you and another for a morsel of energy. Whomever wins gets to keep it. This is why when you're around depressed people; you feel drained. It literally is an energy drain. This is the way the game is played.

In the practice of silence, you change the rules. You don't play to win so you never get caught up in the energy tug of war. Your goal is to understand, enabling exploration, growth and experience. This doesn't mean you don't 'win' occasionally. It just means that the primary focus of your relationships and communication isn't to compete but rather find common ground for mutual understanding. From all appearances, it's a passive perspective. But you may find through practice that, in many ways it's a stronger position than any of the others with less ego baggage.

Exercise

First day: Plan about an hour and a half each day for this exercise. Gather your favorite meal and eat as you always do but pay attention to your thoughts at the time. Write about your experiences using the levels of thought framework from earlier in the chapter.

Second day: See to it that there are no distractions or at the least, minimal distractions. Gather your favorite meal and take it to your favorite spot. Take a moment to remind yourself that something else had to sacrifice in order for you to survive and be grateful (not guilty) for that. Allow yourself to feel the Earth's connection in the simple act of eating. Ask the foods permission to become part of you. Allow yourself to be aware of your senses in relation to your food—the look, the smell, the texture, the temperature, the sound, etc. Give yourself permission to enjoy them. How does it feel to chew, swallow, and digest? How do you feel being a part of the process? Remind yourself that you are receiving it into your system and making it a part of you in the most intimate sense. Become aware in the fullest possible sense. Write about your experience and compare it with the day before. How and why were they different?

Last Words

The answer to the last question is simple. On the first day you were not focused on communicating with yourself or your Creator. On the second day you were. Through questioning and realization you created the bridges that your thoughts needed to become experience. How much more nurturing and fulfilling was the second day than the first? How about the rest of the day? Did that experience ripple into other experiences throughout the day? I guarantee that no matter what you end up with from all this, you'll never look at eating the same way again. After participating in this particular exercise several times, I began to view a lot of things differently. This exercise will help you build the pathways necessary to learn effective communication, not only with but through yourself. If you sift even deeper through levels, you will find even more valuable insights unique to you. Real communication on any level must begin here to provide an accurate foundation for understanding.

Journal Space

Chapter Three

What Stops Us

First Words

This chapter is designed to explore how learning and change shape our lives and thought patterns. I will also outline common personal limitations, things that rob energy, and how to combat energy loss in the moment to moment life.

Material Preparation:	Extra paper Two weeks to take notes (half hour a day approx.) Reflection time

The Pattern of Learned Behavior

Wise ones throughout the ages have said that the difference between knowledge and wisdom is experience. When I heard this, I didn't understand but I felt a truth in it. I had to start thinking about what experience really is. It seemed amusing at the time. Any grade school child knows what experience is but think about it for just a moment.

For example: A person has no other desire but to heal the sick. To do this, they must go to school where they learn to identify, categorize, and treat. These are all the basic steps and 'how tos' of healing. Perhaps they've even worked on a few people. However, until they are practicing what they have learned, they know nothing. The desire to heal drives them, the knowledge supports them but accomplishes little else. Continual exposure, trial and error build a foundation for experience.

As I began to teach others to heal themselves, I kept coming back to my own development and finding more stuff I hadn't seen before, new areas to explore. Some things I didn't know I knew until I had to explain them to someone else. I found that the more I shared the more I learned. That became the basis for experience to flourish.

Because I knew my own behavior patterns, I began to see them in other people and the differences in how they used them as opposed to how I did. I also began to see how basics are woven throughout everyone. I began to extract common patterns and distill them into concepts that act as pivot points in most people though we all use them differently. That built more experience, much as a doctor whose practiced pediatrics for twenty years sees the same type of things over and over only ever so slightly different. The more a given pattern is repeated, the more likely it is to be recognized. When the brain registers recognition, it chemically imprints the pattern for future reference. This is one of the wonders of the physical condition to me.

A baby, when first given solid food, will experiment with it. There's no conscious goal for a baby except the food. I watched as a friend of mine gave her granddaughter a plate of spaghetti. She was about a year or so then. Everyone else was munching away and she was becoming irritated at not being included. So my friend set the plate in front of her and puts the spoon in her hand. With appropriate motions, she showed the child how to feed herself.

When the child became upset, she quickly swept the offending plate and spoon away, offered the child a plate of long strings of spaghetti and a spoon and promptly ignored the child while she finished her own meal. The child picked up the spoon and, watching everyone else, tried to use it in the same way without getting any food. After a few more unsuccessful attempts, she abandoned it in favor of fingers that were easier to control.

Stealing a quick glance to see if she was about to be corrected, she began to experiment. What did the spaghetti look like on her plate, in her hair, and on the floor? What did it feel like when she squished it around on her plate, in her mouth, up her nose, in her hair, and on her shirt? After she'd fully explored the nuances and was satisfied with her results, she settled for simply eating it with her fingers. After exhaustive trials she understood it was the only way to get the food into her mouth. Repetition with similar results transformed the trial and error into recorded experience. Had she not been allowed to explore what she needed to, she wouldn't have understood, she would have simply been following the reactions of others to avoid unpleasant consequences.

Children explore much easier than adults because they haven't learned enough about fear yet. The only thing that will prevent them from exploring is someone else. By the time they reach two or so, they've accumulated enough information about fear and caution that they begin to limit their exploration to more acceptable parameters to avoid punishment. However, often this is in conflict with what they really want and the results of this internal tug-of-war come out in their behavior.

The way someone perceives punishment has a lot to do with the make up of their personality and it starts in the first few years. It also determines how a person will relate to fear. Why? The pattern has repeated enough to record a specific message in the brain on how fear should be used to control behavior and perceive the world. This, in turn, as the individual grows becomes reactional. Little thought is involved in simple response to stimuli. In fact, one need take no responsibility for their actions or consequences if they are 'forced' into it. In these cases there is no understanding because there's no choice. Simply a chain of learned behavior that follows and limits them throughout their lives.

Identifying the Chains:

It begins at birth. New eyes peek at a blurry collage of sights and sounds; listening for the voices it knows from before everything in its world changed. It was warm; now it's not. It was relatively dark, now. It's bright. There's too much room for movement and suddenly a new response kicks in; the first breath of a newborn infant and everything it has ever known changed forever.

To the parents, it's everything they could've hoped for, an event they will cherish for the rest of their lives. Today, everything changes for them as well. They're parents, stewards to a new life that will depend on them in various ways for the rest of their lives. For both parties—in different ways, they have moved from a place of safety and security headfirst into the unknown in every way imaginable.

The baby is now independent of its mother physically. It is no longer being fed at all times from the cord so it now must gain attention for food. It is no longer cushioned from pain by the water of her womb. If the child flails his arms and hits the side of the crib, it hurts—another new sensation. Clothing replaces the warmth of the mother's body and most important everything sounds different. The comforting sound of her steady muffled heartbeat is heard only in the brief moments of cuddling and then disappears. In its place, there are new sharper sounds, no longer gently shadowed by a watery environment. From birth, a child will seek replacements for what was lost while in the security of the womb and bond to those things both biochemically and emotionally as a matter of survival.

The child has few clues to the existence of an outside environment, the voices of the parents and friends they've heard often. I'll never forget sitting with my newborn watching the daytime shows and his head whipped around in recognition of a theme song. Food becomes a focal point of the bonding experience. There is a nurturing to the first experiences of eating in addition to the biochemical responses of the child's brain, totally independent for the first time. Warmth is another factor. For some time now, hospitals have wrapped newborns tightly in the receiving blankets to simulate the warmth and closeness of the womb to ease the transition. All of these things help a newborn to adapt to the outside world and carry over some of the security it had known before the big change. All these things help to set the foundation for everything that child will learn in life and how they will learn it. Why? It's the first time they have experienced the reality of change.

Physical Change

Organic life is a self-sustaining system once put into motion. It's built to accept change on every level, what we call adaptation. After a series of comparable, successful adaptations, we learn. The experience of learning is growth.

Biochemically the body is a stimulus oriented supply and demand loop. As vulnerable and fragile as a baby may seem, it is often better equipped to handle change than are adults because they haven't been conditioned by their psychology to respond in specific ways yet. They have no expectations of any particular outcome to a given stimulus and will experiment to find out what works best. Any parent will tell you that there are different cries for different needs and in a way, the baby trains the parent to listen for a particular request by repeating what worked before. The body works in the same way.

Input creates processing and output. Food creates digestion, excretion, energy, and storage. No food and the rest keep going as long as it can with what it's got until the system fails for lack of input. A hand strays to a hot burner and creates an emergency signal from the nervous system spreading adrenaline throughout the body to fix the problem by empowering the nervous system before conscious awareness even kicks in.

It's the very anatomy of how we learn and retain information. That reaction is stored in a chemical library of information within our brains so that we may avoid unpleasant and harmful situations (protection) or retain the ability to enjoy a similar experience. No matter where it begins, what happens on one level will invade all the others in an attempt to balance the system. This is why true and lasting healing of any kind is about balance.

The brain is the computer for all the information that is processed and the body is the clearing house for what is recorded from there. As a baby, stimulus and response create a neural pathway and something is learned. A pain in the stomach results in a rousing cry for input or food to fuel the system. The proper cry produces results. Food is introduced and the physical processes continue until the next time. Deep within the child's brain, neural energy roamed until it found a compatible chemical receptor that connected stimuli with response.

Each time that pain is experienced, the neural energy will travel the pathway that produced results. Each time it has similar results, the pathway receives more receptors to reinforce the behavior and ensure favorable results and thus overall survival of the entire system. Any deviation creates stress to that pathway and the need to find a new pathway that works. Say that the mother had to do shopping and so the baby got lunch a bit late. A new pathway is created and something new is learned, but it only happens when a previous behavior doesn't produce successful results. Sometimes it's merely a modification to a previous pathway. The stimulus is still pain in the stomach but the situation has changed creating the need for a different set of responses.

Once calculated in the brain through a chemistry of trial and error, those surviving chemical messengers communicate to the rest of the system about what needs to be done to insure balance. Food is introduced, and a result produces a new stimulus. The inflow of food needs to be processed and distributed or the system can become unbalanced. Cells need to be built and replaced, blood needs to travel, muscles need to be supplied, waste needs to be eliminated. The brain has already communicated these particular needs to various systems through balancing its own loops and the imbalance tells it what it needs. If it remains unbalanced, the health and life of the cell is in jeopardy. The individual cell sends out its own messengers to talk to the main system transporters, as you would talk to an operator to make an overseas call. The main system transporters either stimulate or shut down nerve pathways according to what is needed to balance the system. The nervous system communicates to the brain through this chemical phone call and the brain responds to regain balance. When the brain balances its own chemicals properly, it releases the appropriate chemicals until it gets the signal to stop because the system is balanced. Then the entire system plateaus until stimuli are introduced again. The baby is no longer hungry, the physical requirements are satisfied and the message ripples throughout his body to stop demanding. He stops crying, goes to sleep and gradually the whole process will begin again. When everything is working ideally, his body will work to balance and sustain himself his entire life in the same way.

However, what appears to be a blessing to ensure survival on the most elementary of levels can be a curse as the physical patterns ripple and expand into behaviors and emotions. We all know the person who enters into the same situations over and over again and gets trashed every time. I've been studying various forms of abuse for ten years, specifically within relationships and the story is always the same. We all know the addictive person who goes back to the bottle or cigarette knowing it isn't good for them, but being unable to break the cycle. Any addictive behavior uses the same process of experimentation and recognition to imprint the pattern into the brain's neural net.

Emotional Change

What is true for one level usually expands to others. Here we need to separate the addictive personalities from the non addictive ones. Addictive personalities have one coping mechanism for change, escapism.

This is a chicken or egg argument in some cases. Which came first, the chemistry or the behavior? Most of the time it's triggered by a logic loop of sorts deep within the persona. A pattern is recognized and worked but with uncertain or unstable results. This creates void leading to stress in systems on whatever level the stress happens. Unable to complete the pattern, the person will seek a substitute to fill the void to resolve the loop but by then the stress reaction is in the chemistry. For example: A man in emotional pain. Instead of seeking out a way to understand and cope with his pain, he drinks to forget the problem, a temporary solution at best but a resolution to the logic loop nonetheless. The logic loop: to stop the pain caused by change. The chemistry of the body accepts this as a solution because the emotional pain does stop. This feeds his desire to use this as a coping mechanism building a physical dependency to support it. By the time it reaches the level of physical dependency, it isn't possible to change the behavior solely through psychology. At that point, intervention and support are needed. The drive to complete the physical dependency cycle virtually takes over the person in an attempt to feed itself.

In non addictive personalities it's a slightly different story. Example: Someone you love dies suddenly. Your physical body will register distress. Why? *Emotional shock freezes neural activity at the point that the shock was registered.* This is a protective feature of the human emotional condition. The change is so immediate and pervasive that the actual chemistry hasn't caught up to itself. The remaining neural energy keeps bumping into the last thing it was receiving, i.e., you keep reliving the same moment over and over. Since the natural process of the body is to flow whether it's blood, neural energy, chemical exchanges, etc. any time, for whatever reason, a flow is stopped suddenly an injury is perceived by the entire system and it struggles to balance itself. Digestion is slowed, perception is intensified, all but essential systems are slowed to a trickle and all the efforts reduce damage to the system and insure continuation once things even out.

The imbalance occurs when the person isn't allowed for whatever reason, to cope with the shock and heal. They literally cannot get past it no matter how much they want to because the mechanisms for protection are still in force. The neural energy is still bumping up against the block; the person keeps reliving the trauma and the loops begin to work against them instead of for them by creating fear and suspicion as a coping method to prevent the injury from happening again. This creates a continual path of stress related adaptations to any situation that relates to similar traumas. You become reactionary.

This is most evident in cases where the trauma hits all levels at once; specifically wars, abuse, deaths and the crimes associated with such traumas. These are pervasive and long ranging traumas with precious little time to adapt. The more levels of existence are affected, the greater the response to the trauma. The body's chemical messengers struggle to protect instead of heal and the more the message is repeated, the greater the pathway established. Pretty soon, you interpret everything as a threat you must protect yourself from. A negative attitude is established and continues until a reason to change occurs. It's a tough climb from this point because the drive for survival is so strong. Either protection or healing will insure continuance but, if given the choice, most would choose protection over healing as a way of life. A combination of both will establish a balance.

All that said and done, we aren't completely victims of our physical processes either. Our desire to change an existing condition stimulates chemical messengers as well. Once the remnants of trauma are balanced out, a flow can be reestablished and redirected to learn as well build a form of immunity against the impact of a similar trauma. The negative behaviors can be taught how to heal and redirected into positive behavior. But it doesn't happen by itself, you have to want the change even if you don't really know how you want it to change. In the strict anatomy of it all, wanting to change is half the battle. Once recognized it begins to transform. Why?

Imagine you are descending steps to a basement you know to be full of living things. The lights don't work so the further you go, the more darkness there is. You have no idea what's there so when you reach the bottom, it's likely that you'll trip on things until you know where they're at. Even then, things down there are always moving around so unless you can find a way to see in absolute darkness, you can't be effective. Desire, is like taking a flashlight with you into the darkness. Once you see something, you can choose. Once choice is applied, things change. Why? Because once you recognize choice and exercise it you go from reactive to active. It shifts everything from a negative flow of the victim to a positive flow of participant.

Power Suckers

Anything that takes energy away from you or wastes it on a consistent basis is what I call a power sucker. These are limitations that you place, either consciously or through habit, on the cycle of change within the context of your life.

Now I ask you, if you had a 100-watt bulb and insisted on feeding it 150 watts in hopes that 100 watts would get to you faster or better, what would happen? You'd burn out the bulb and probably wreck your house. Not to mention it would be ridiculous to even contemplate, right? Now, if you had that 100-watt bulb and gave it only 50 watts of energy while expecting the same 100-watt performance from it, that equally ridiculous, right?

Imagine you are a 100-watt bulb designed to give off 100 watts of ambient, warm light. Subtract 50 watts for every category you are proficient in.

Fear /- 50 watts

When you come face to face with perceived helplessness in any form, there is a fear. When you come face to face with the unexpected, there may be fear. When you come face to face with the unknown, there may be fear. But what exactly is it?

Fear Behaviors

Example: Suzy and Bill have known each other for many years. Just friends, mind you, nothing more. Not that Bill wouldn't like it to be more but he's scared that if he approached Suzy, she would reject him and that would change the friendship. Worse yet, if they became more and it didn't work out, there may not be a friendship afterward. So Bill chose to stay quiet. He thought he was protecting the friendship he couldn't bear to lose but what he was really doing was feeding a fear that will eventually get out of control. How?

Well, I'm sure it's plain to anyone not in this predicament what the trouble is. It's not so easy when you're in the grip of fear to see anything but what it wants you to see. Bill suffers many things at once. First, a lack of trust of Suzy. If their friendship is that strong, it will survive his overtures should she not be interested. If it isn't to survive, then perhaps he's laboring under an illusion about their relationship. If that was the case, the friendship wouldn't survive Suzy's first real love anyway. Second, he suffers from a lack of self esteem. They should've talked about it long before he developed a fear.

Perhaps he felt he was protecting her feelings. Big man. Big mistake. It's still a lack of trust for Suzy. She would benefit far more from the truth then some illusionary world he held up for her. Again, the relationship would end and probably badly as Suzy woke up to the real world.

There are things we do need to protect ourselves from. Sometimes it's a rotten world. But love is seldom one we need protection from.

Bill could be suffering from a past traumatic remembrance. Maybe this had happened to him before where he professed his love and was rejected. So now, to protect himself from the pain of loss, he suffers in silence the fear he cannot express. Poor Bill, a victim of his own fear. Helpless? No. Not by a long shot.

I used this example in an effort to illustrate how fear is disguised as acceptable and even expected social and personal behavior. Plays and timeless love stories have been written for centuries using this very plot. Society is conditioned to believe that this is the way we should treat ourselves and each other. It's romantic. See how much he loves her. He hides his true emotion to spare her the burden. How ridiculous does that sound in the light of understanding?

Every day, countless people rise with the sun and begin the lament of fear. 'What will I wear' translates into—(fear language) 'What will people think of me if I wear this?' I can't do that because this will happen, a.k.a. the great 'What If'; the interjection of the unknown into somewhere you don't want or flatly refuse to make a choice.

So What is Fear—Really

This is a question I've wrestled with for some time now. No matter where I looked within myself, I couldn't really pin down what it was. I knew I felt it from time to time but what was it really? When I looked at the biochemistry of trauma, I noticed something. Anywhere I looked regarding fear, all the elements of the experience had one thing in common. Fear is perceived when something inside you stops. From there I realized that fear is the interruption of the natural flow of whatever level you're looking at. It's like placing a dam in the middle of the stream. How large the dam was, determined the continuation of the flow. This creates disparate levels of interference. In one situation you may have a lot of fear and in others, you will only have a little bit. The stream represents the flow of energy from your spirit to your body. Where that is stopped, creates damage on the physical level. Why?

Your physical body depends on much more than a collection of physical responses. How many times in the last week have you referred to not having enough energy to do something? When you say that, what are you talking about? If food was the only source of energy a body receives then when you eat you should be fully charged and yet more often than not, that isn't the case. The same is true for oxygen and sunlight. If that was all it took, we'd be at100 percent whenever we undertook a series of physical steps to produce that result. We would heal instantly in hospitals once the proper elements were replaced and yet none of this is the case.

So there must be another source of energy that sustains and supports life, a force of life like in Star Wars. That's the flow of life from Creator to us, the source of the stream. Remember always that the nature of the stream is a flow that will in turn create change. Whether backwards or forwards, it will always flow so long as we're alive. When that flow is obstructed it backs up and, after a time, reverses bio-electrical polarity like a stream running backwards. The physical body is no longer receiving that energy to sustain the life within the cell. The cell becomes damaged and, once a negative flow is dominating in that area, an energy vacuum is created similar to a black hole. The key to being able to control this within yourself is awareness and application of choice beginning with First Choice. The stream is provided; you choose what to do with it! Only you can move your arms and legs. Bear in mind that fear is not the enemy, your willingness to believe and feed it is.

It may not seem like much on the surface, pie in the sky wishful thinking. But consider the implications in practice for a moment. What room is there for fear in the face of real awareness of choice? There would be room for the caution and discernment necessary for the fight or flight reality of survival but no room for the effect of fear.

Ownership of Fear(regain 50 watts)

Fear itself is an unstable force when unsupported. Many people don't know this, but it's true. It is most strong when you continually feed it bits and pieces of your power by letting fear make the choices for you. If you turn away from it, it becomes stronger because you are, in a sense, trying to convince yourself fear doesn't exist. Well, if it doesn't exist—why do you need convincing? If you fight it, it becomes stronger. By fighting, you validate it's right to be and fight for that morsel of energy contained in choice. In a way, fear is telling you not to choose.

Confrontation is the only way to gain control over it. Look deeply into it. Believe it or not, sometimes that's all it takes to own it. Challenge it and challenge yourself. It's there to teach you something about yourself. Ask it and learn then use that knowledge to choose in the light of understanding.

The only time fear exists is where choice has not been exercised on either a personal or situational level. You may not be able to do anything about the situation but you can choose how it will affect you, especially on the emotional level. If you need proof, look at actor Christopher Reeves' example. He built a career from the portrayal of the comic book character Superman. In one moment, his entire life changed from one of relative freedom to one of almost complete paralysis. Where he could do for himself, now he must rely on others for the most basic of day to day tasks. He could spend every waking moment afraid that he will not be able to breathe in the next but he doesn't. He could've just holed up in his home and shut out the public, safe in his private world and he didn't. No matter what circumstances have handed this guy he's turned it to his advantage and never let it beat him permanently. Truly Superman. Incredibly, he took it further by reaching out to helping others by advocating and supporting research into paralysis. He had his moments, I'm sure, but he chooses how to handle it and how it would affect him on a personal level. There are countless others with stories just as compelling as his. That's where the transformation begins. That's the source of strength, deep within. Ironically, you demonstrate who you really are the first time you turn to face down your fear and win. It lends new truth to the saying,

"The only thing we have to fear is fear itself."
Franklin Delano Roosevelt

Expectation/-50 watts

A demand of personal power exerted toward a future goal is what we call expectation. As we will discuss later, some expectations are healthy. I don't dispute that. If you work, you should look forward to getting paid. However, I see far more of the expectation I'm going to illustrate.

Expectation takes on many forms, useful and not so useful. The types of expectation that put undue pressure upon you are the ones not serving you. Likely as not, they will be self imposed. If you want to know what those are, look at your life and find where you put the blame for not meeting preconceived expectations.

An example from my own life: It comes back to this book actually. You are reading the culmination of years of personal work on myself but to you, it looks like it happened all at once. For a time, I printed and published it myself and sold it over the Internet. To date, it's been very fulfilling but a slow business. Finding anything over the Internet, much less selling it is like a needle in the proverbial haystack for a minuscule independent. To date, I'm still overseas where American places are few and far between so independent bookstores have also been a challenge. So I made a decision to go with the publisher from which you likely bought the one you're holding, in order to get a mass market distribution.

Long story short, the word count of the book was too small for the type of binding required by the publisher, so I had to add to the original manuscript. Not a problem since I'd already started on a companion book on the 'how to' of healing. But in trying to piece the two together, it didn't make any sense. I began to feel pressure. What I'd worked for was within my grasp and yet so far away…it was driving me nuts!

What you will eventually read isn't too different from the original but embodies what I'd originally envisioned for the first of the series. However, it required me to get around a few of my own expectations to accomplish it. I created pressure and, self imposed as it was, it robbed me of the ability to think and follow through. Why? What did I expect? There was the thousand-dollar question. What did I expect? By the same method I use to challenge a fear, I turned on my expectations and actually, simply—unbelieved them. It worked! Seems it's only power expectation had was the belief that I placed in its existence.

When I found that there wasn't anything actually there I was shocked. So what was the pressure I'd been feeling? What I should be doing, what others thought I was going to do…and on and on. 'When are you going to get a real job and give up on that book? Or that look I'd get when people ask you what you do and you say, I'm a writer. They look at you like you should be 'more.' I blamed them and myself for not being and behaving in a way they found adequate. In this instance blame was taking the form of expectation, looking to the future when I wouldn't feel inadequate anymore because I accomplished what I set out to do in spite of what I thought they thought. The pressure was from wanting to be there so much, I was in a hurry and afraid I wouldn't meet it. Expectation takes on some interesting interpersonal loops as it unravels. I was that 100-watt bulb trying desperately to shine on only 50 watts of power.

Combating Expectation(regain 50 watts)

Who do you blame? That will tell you where your energy is going in thoughts and fears. You blame the teacher—it's going there. You blame your parents—it's going there. You blame yourself—it's leaking out there. When there's pressure—that feeling like you are pushing a Cadillac with your nose, uphill in the winter—there will likely be blame. When the strain feels like you're 'fighting the good fight' and just being yourself—it's everyone else with the problem…that's blame and personal energy is focused outward toward a target. Know who, what or where the blame is going first.

Where there is blame there will be emotional distress of some variety. Injury in the form of anger, hurt, indifference, or fear are the usual suspects. They perform the warrior work to protect punctured emotions from being damaged further. Allowing these reactions to continue unchecked and unresolved causes expectation, beginning the cycle all over again. Instead of reacting to these conditions, learn to act through and defy these phantoms. Instead of blaming, act to understand. Instead of anger, act to learn from experiences. Instead of fear, act to broaden your conscious awareness. Instead of giving your power to circumstances, reclaim your power in the action of choice.

Self Punishment/-50 watts

If I take responsibility for something that is within my sphere of influence and act on it accordingly, this transforms into a conscious awareness of the actions and consequences of what I set into motion. If I blame myself for participation in something that was within my peripheral awareness—I'm punishing myself. There is an important difference. One is constructive, one is destructive but it isn't always easy to tell. Some people are craftier than others at disguising one for the other. It's a difficult nut to crack without directly looking at the dynamics of the mechanism.

Example: I have a friend who blames herself for the death of someone she loved very much. This person took his own life but she has never gotten past the 'if only'. If only she'd been there. If only she'd known he was that close to doing it. If only she could've prevented it. It's a bitter thing to live with and 'if only'. Her spirit is frozen in that torment, refusing to move past it. To keep herself there, she blames herself. What's happening?

We live, we die—fundamentally. We live and we feel empowered by life, no matter how small the degree. In death, we feel helpless. That is at the heart of self punishment. Wherever you experience that feeling of impotence, you will punish yourself. Why? It gives you the illusion you are doing something about it and symbolically combats the powerlessness.

Sometimes it's to keep a situation current. Were she to move past the pain, past the what ifs—then he'd truly be gone. She couldn't stop him from dying but she will stop him from leaving her, so she uses this punishment as a way to keep herself in the pain and in effect, keep him alive.

Sometimes it's to protect the pain. If you're involved with punishing yourself—you never need devote energy to the pain. If you never need to acknowledge or feel the pain; you can again stay right where you have the illusion of control.

Sometimes a person may feel they deserve it or owe it to the person who died, eternal responsibility for an imaginary crime. Under these conditions, two people die, one just looks alive.

Pain is an interesting thing though. Its natural state isn't permanent—it's changing. It cannot sustain an energy for long periods of time. If they want to keep the pain alive, they have to nourish it. This is where you assume the illusion of control. In reality, you're only directing the regulation of the pain but it will appear that you're in command of the situation. This is why people who consistently punish themselves seem embittered at the world. People with habitually negative personalities are feeding it frequently to keep it in an assiduous state.

Ownership (regain 50 watts)

To break the illusion and bring your life into choice again, you must go through the pain and come out the other side. You must feel it, accept that you are feeling it, choose to feel it. No one likes to hear this much less endure the experience. Let's face it, pain hurts! Unchecked pain is a demanding master. It will demand you time, your thoughts, your energy and your health. It's so much more potent when you are doing it to yourself.

One of the things I do is push it to be more than it is. If I'm feeling depressed, I chose to be the best depressed person in the history of the world. No one will be more depressed than I am! I will be the queen of depression. People will bow to the superiority of my lackluster inclinations. When I begin to think like this, it sounds pretty silly. The trivializing of what has become magnified to the point of distortion helps put a more realistic perspective on the experience and strengthens your emotional immunity against it happening again.

So what does going through the pain really mean? How do you know when you're through? Choice is emotional illumination. Once you choose and feel, it begins to change. Sure it hurts but it will change as more light circulates. Like an unfamiliar road that is dark, the twists and turns can throw you. Gradually though, the radiance transforms the darkness and your pain adapts to the new energy conditions. The effects that begin in thought and emotion ripple throughout your physical body sending chemical messengers to support a new matrix of thought, a new pattern of learning.

Judgment/-50 watts

What is it? Christ said, "Judge not lest ye be judged." Have you ever wondered why? Lets use an example: You're driving to work, in a hurry because you pushed your snooze and slept too late. Not paying attention you pull out in front of someone and miss them by a few inches. The person in the other car, reasonably upset chooses to display his feelings with a socially understandable symbol of disgust, irritation and judgment of your apparent character. Now you are upset. You didn't mean it. It was a mistake and you're being unfairly judged for it. Certainly you would never react that way! You would be understanding.

I love this particular example because it's not something typically thought of as judgment. But lets look at the anatomy of it for a moment from both sides.

Your side: Your choices led to your participation in the situation. How? You chose to roll over and go back to sleep causing your tardiness. You also chose to rush around instead of being a little late to work and exercising the usual caution on the road. The dam of your flow is built around this moment by refusing to accept your responsibilities. If you had been aware of your choices and really looked at the situation instead of having your eyes only on the fear generated by arriving to work late, you could've changed the situation with different choices. Instead, by rushing around, you placed someone else in the position of being responsible for your lack of choices.

Re-enforcing the dam, you become upset by the other drivers' reaction and blame him for his lack of understanding. This is a classic example of what is called mirroring. This is what Christ was talking about. You will *always* judge someone else for something you do not want to see in yourself. He wasn't speaking of His judgment; he was warning us of our own. It is a BIG clue to what's going on inside your spirit and a powerful tool if used to become aware rather than ignored. Any time you are judging someone else you are seeing something within yourself you don't like. If you don't recognize it, you become a victim of 'misunderstanding idiots' like the one who judged you in the first place and in effect, you've become just like them. "Judge not lest ye be judged." The Ego moves to save itself by re-enforcing the illusion that you are better in order to enable further judgment. "I would never do that. I would be understanding." As a direct challenge to that illusion, if you would be more understanding then why not be in the moment? You have paid a price for your lack of choice in self-esteem and personal growth.

Their side: Their choices also led to this moment. Perhaps it wasn't lack of responsibility on their part. Suppose that everything was going just as they planned. They read the paper, drank 2.5 cups of coffee, dressed in starched shirt and pleated slacks and headed out to meet the day. They did everything responsibly and with awareness of choice and still have to deal with rouges like you. They are just as much a victim.

What if they had chosen to skip the paper and get to work early. They likely wouldn't have been there at the same time you were being irresponsible. They could've been safe in the illusion that they were perfect and in control.

But life doesn't allow for much of that. Choices must be made and more often then not they conflict with the choices made by others. For that, they become angry at you for shattering their illusion of control and flip you the bird instead of recognizing where their choices lead to that moment as well. By choosing to be angry they forfeit their ability to learn about their choices from the event and they lose the opportunity to learn about themselves and develop greater compassion. As far as they are concerned it was all your fault and they've let you know it. Their thought on the matter is closed and a dam in the flow is built. Later in the day, little things will build upon that block and create a negative flow. After a while, they find they are having a lousy day and without knowing why. They will blame it on the idiot that pulled out in front of them for starting the downhill slide. They too have paid a price by surrendering choice to blame and illusion.

Situation with choice: Let's say that both parties arrive in the same moment through the choices they have made. However this time, instead of blaming each other they look at themselves. Instead of judging and elevating themselves, they use the event as an opportunity to learn about themselves and life. The chain of personal impact is broken and growth prevails. Positive balances out the negative and understanding becomes a part of them. The situation doesn't change, how they use it does. How powerful a force in your life could this be if every time you judged someone you used it as an opportunity to see yourself instead of just blaming the other guy? How much of life are you missing because of it? How much of yourself are you missing? How high a price are you paying?

All of life is an opportunity to grow. All of life is an opportunity to die. The CHOICE is yours. Never deny your feelings, use them to understand yourself. If you are upset then be upset but don't be satisfied with only that. Grow from adversity. Challenge the truth you think you see. Nothing real can be threatened. If it's true, you will grow from it not be a victim of it. When you can do this, there will be no room for fear to control you. Without fear there is no room for judgment. Without judgment there is no room for suspicion and doubt. Negativity ceases to inhibit your natural flow and you begin living instead of simply existing.

Exercise

Ownership (regain 50watts)

It's simple. Choose to look at everyone in your life as a mirror of yourself and use it to learn. Everyone—children, parents, colleagues, spouses, friends and enemies. What you see in them is what you see in yourself, good and bad. As the world is a stage and we are mere actors—people in your life are aspects of yourself finding voice and for the first time you choose to listen. If you find some revelation unpleasant, challenge it, choose to change yourself and become stronger from the experience. This will prevent you from falling into the victim mind set. If change is the reining force in life then nothing is set in stone. Even the oldest, most ingrained patterns can be changed if the individual wants to. If something feels like it stops you, choose to see it and grow from it. Fear cannot exist in the light of choice. They are mutually exclusive.

Do this for two weeks keeping a daily journal. Be diligent because it's important to record your inner processing in case you get lost and need to see where you got off track.

When the two weeks are up, answer the questions from Chapter One again. Don't look at the previous answers, just answer them now. After you finish, then compare them with your previous answers. How are they different? How are they the same as before? What are you learning from the comparison?

Last Words

Take notice of what's happening around you. I know when I went through this, situations didn't change right away but began to change as I moved away from my fear related reactions and into choice. In fact I was rather surprised that it did and decided to do my best to figure out why. Logically, I was the only one that should be changed since the others around me were making the same choices or lack of choices they made before but that isn't what happened. My husband's stress leveled out and my kids didn't fight nearly as much as before. Even strangers that came into my life tended to be different somehow. And yet, nothing outside myself had actually changed! It boggled my mind.

Imagine a stressful situation as an agreement between you and someone else to tug on separate ends of a rope until someone wins. The best that can be hoped for realistically is more of the same game over and over again, neither party giving in nor giving up. So what if you choose to let go and find another way? What happens to the one pulling on the other end? What happens to the game? That was why things and people were changing around me, I wasn't playing the game anymore and because everything is connected, everything changed right along with me. My husband still gets stressed with other people but not with me. I don't play to win anymore; I play to understand. That way we both win. And that's just a small example of how it works. But let me be the first to tell you—it isn't easy.

I had a dream once that I was a reluctant tennis ball in a rather rowdy game of tennis. I was being beaten up between two forces and I didn't see any way out until I spied the net. I reached out and grabbed the net and clung there until the two players came over to see why their ball was hanging there. One tried to pluck me from the net but I hung tenaciously refusing to go. The other player looked at me and, with a rather vicious grin said, "Do you get it now?" Then I abruptly woke and began to understand what I'd been trying to see. The social game is about who's better and who will win because of it. Refuse to play the game and you take control back, you take choice back, you empower your life.

Journal Space

Chapter Four

Identity

First Words

This is a richly complex chapter designed to take you from the illusions of the work-a-day world to the truth of the inner world of awareness. Through the subjects of fear and conformity, we will explore how and why identities develop for groups and affect the individual. The exercise at the end of the chapter will take you on a journey from the workings outside, inward to your core-self.

Material Preparation:	Notes from Chapter One
	A long tape of enjoyable music
	Time

In Chapter One I asked you to ponder a question without answering it, who are you? This chapter will delve deeply into what that question means for the answer is worth nothing without that understanding.

All the questions in Chapter One help to reveal your current state of mind and how you relate to yourself on all levels. But are any of these answers who you are? Question One of the physical—What do my eyes see? Hopefully in the literal sense you saw a person. If not than perhaps you need a good plastic surgeon or maybe a new pair of glasses. Those who nurture a desire to grow and attention to detail may have listed various observations based on appearance and mood. But is this who you are?

Question One of the Mental—What do I think I know? This is a question to gauge not only your level of self confidence but your awareness of your capabilities and general mental stability. But does your answer reveal who you are?

Question One of the Emotional—What do I feel about myself? This question addresses what you tell yourself emotionally. It is a hint to the inner tapes that play constantly in everyone's mind modifying behavior patterns to match the moment. But does it tell you who you are?

You may be surprised that most people will answer yes to the question, but it doesn't hold up when you begin to examine it deeply. In truth, none of the answers to these questions will provide you with the answer to who you are. All these answers are identification points. They are tools we use to measure ourselves against the people and thoughts we love, hate, or respect. They're also the tools that ultimately everyone else will use to understand us. But are they who you really are?

The question of who you are is a completely different perspective than that of how you're identified. How you're identified is what others use to find you in a world full of various sensory inputs. Without identification points there would be no commonality for communication or frames of reference for experience. The difficulty in life comes when you take these identification points and make them who you are.

A litany of creative mental illness that find their beginnings here. Stress—Co-dependence—various addictions—the entire range of reactionary behavior—paranoia, etc. They are all products of the ever adaptable mind trying to cope with or escape the discrepancy between what it knows internally, and what it's receiving externally. When it cannot be balanced, the mind extrapolates available information and emotional input from you (perceived as past experience) and creates a likely picture of who you are and what's going on. It's as simple as a twist of thought to break that cycle. When you ask who you are, put the accent and focus on the who in the sentence.

Universal Identities

There are emotionally based identities that can be said of everyone in society that fall into several categories: failure, success, controlling, traumatic, and conformity. Though you will find these categories on a somewhat individual level as well, they mostly appear where fear is present in groups of people. You can use these generalities to find where you 'stopped' your personal energy in a given situation.

Failure

The general explanation of failure is to fall short of success. Now take the actual idea of failure out of the social concept and into simplicity. To fall short is to be less. So failure is less than success. That, when applied in emotional terms to the self means that you are less when you fail by our own social definitions. However, there is a loophole.

Begin by peeling off the layers of illusion that have built up from the attempt to protect yourself and cope with your childhood environment. Even the best of homes and families have symptoms of this illusionary type of plaque passed on from generation to generation. Start with what you think you know about yourself and challenge the truth of it.

For example: Lets assume that as a child, you labored under the impression, either directly or inadvertently, that you weren't living up to the expectations of those you were surrounded by. When you look in the mirror, perhaps you see failure and no doubt you have a list as long as your arm to prove it. So did I. The key is to challenge it, don't justify it or place blame. Ask yourself, IS IT TRUTH, or is it something you accepted without questioning.

Think back to the first memory of feeling failure and challenge that. Did you really fail or perhaps, more simply, had a lot to learn? Look for the truth in what you've taken in and don't stop till you find it. Don't be satisfied till you have the whole picture. I guarantee you that every negative, you can find a positive if you really want to. Choose to hunt for what you've learned, what you've gained not just what you've lost.

Please don't mistake this for 'positive thought.' Personally I think that tool is deceptive at best. My approach is about balance and learning not convincing yourself of something you're unwilling to accept in the first place. Growing is what gives the journey value. You must see both to make effective choices and stop the victimizing of yourself through learned behavior attitudes. You can't just take the good or the bad and hope to come out whole in the long run. You must consciously and actively balance them.

This is what I fondly refer to as the Warriors' attitude and will work with all the social identities. If you feel 'victimized' by anything, that is what you turn and challenge. With a little thought and honesty, they aren't usually able to keep their energy. This process is necessary to remove everything that doesn't belong so you can see, like wiping a muddy window.

This becomes more challenging in cases of severe trauma although, if the experience is profound enough and the person is motivated, then it can work. But there has to be an incredible desire on behalf of the injured party for that to occur. Sometimes, it takes a lifetime to understand what an unwanted experience has taught you and/or what you did with it. But if you keep searching, you will eventually understand. You only fail if you stop.

Never give up or settle for an answer that doesn't free you. When you get there you will know. There is an exhilaration of freedom that comes with the experience of a truth and you can feel in every sense that you are no longer entrapped by that pattern anymore. It is unmistakable and profound. I've felt honored to be present when this has happened with some of my friends.

Success

Websters—Success is a favorable outcome or attainment of. To succeed is to accomplish. So to succeed is to complete and/or add to. Fear of success is most interesting because it often masquerades as fear of failure; fear being the primary force behind both.

Both fears share common motivations in that both will protect you from the responsibility of learning and making choices while you run around in their mazes. The method of dispelling illusion and revealing truth are the same. Challenge the truth of the thought.

Example: I'll use myself for this one. If you are reading this book then I have done what I fear the most—succeeded. Every day I sit at the computer I challenge a multitude of fears regarding this book ever going public. Most revolve around what my responsibility in sharing this information will be. What will people expect of me? Who do I think I am, I didn't even go to college? How will it affect my family? What if I'm just making a public fool of myself? What do I know about the publishing business? This is the beginnings of a very long list.

They appear to be failure-fear related but look closer. Fear of failure is socially acceptable. There are few 'winners' on the societal scale. Fear of success is ridiculous. Everyone wants to succeed, right?

I am what is known as a self-saboteur. Just when it looks good, I find some way to mess it up. Why? If this book succeeds then all of this is no longer in my 'imagination' where it can be whatever I want it to be. It's been witnessed by others and taken a life of it's own. And I don't know what will happen to the people it touches. I know it worked for me but what if...and my brain takes off, imagining a multitude of awful and wonderful illusions to protect myself from going any further. Bottom line—I can't control it once it leaves my desk so I stop it with my fears. That's the fear of success hidden in most control freaks.

I find it a lot more common than fear of failure, believe it or not. At heart, people are lazy when it comes to self maintenance, especially in the emotional department. I am no exception. The only difference is that I have challenged my demons. I understand how and why they affect me and made a choice. I stopped victimizing myself.

Control Addicts

These are the people I have the most and least compassion for, being a recovering one myself. I know what it's like to have life brutally rake you across the coals without so much as an apology or bandage. Those to whom this happens at a young age generally go one of two ways: totally into control or totally into denial. The urge to grab the world or a person by the horns and make happen what you will, is the deciding factor in most fear related responses. It's usually traceable to when you had a major trauma event of some kind that invoked an extreme sense of helplessness. The idea of control is to prevent that from ever happening again. If you cannot prevent history from repeating itself, so to speak, you do everything you can to have some say in the emotional outcome.

I say I have the most compassion for this group because these are usually the gentlest souls that for whatever reason didn't have time to adjust to the randomness of life before they were hip deep in the harshness of it all. They have spent a lifetime covering up this tenderness to save what little life is left for them to feel with, As a result, they have the appearance of tough exteriors. I call them the turtle people because I once heard it said that the tough exterior protects the soft inside and it reminded me very much of a turtle; dragging around the weight of its shelter and hiding their true form from all. Not an easy thing to remember when you are the subject of a controlling type of person but true none-the-less.

I have the least compassion for them because people committed to this cycle of energy are using it against themselves. What they can do they can undo, they simply refuse. This is the other extreme of the controller—denial. They either hide and pretend like everything is fine when in reality, everything is falling apart, or they ignore any reaction they are having to the situation insisting again that reality isn't happening.

Both reactions of the controlling person are linked to personal response-ability. One is taking more responsibility than is your due and the other is ignoring responsibility all together. Redefining your perspective of responsibility is crucial to balancing this identity type and finding who you really are, not who you think you have to be.

Response-ability

This concept has taken on so many meanings through the years. I separate it into two words to remind myself what it really means. I may be able to shed light in areas of understanding that help you to see something you couldn't before but you are the only one who can see it for yourself. You are the only one who can respond to the stimuli and then choose if it's for you or not. I cannot do that for you. I've told all the students I've ever had that my only responsibility is availability. Everything else is up to them. As a mother of two with many questions and budding insecurities of what my children's teen years will bring, this simple twist of thought has made all the difference between protecting my children through control or empowering them to respond on their own.

Traumatic Experiences

I recently had an experience that tested all my convictions on choice. My father-in-law died after complications from surgery. My whole family had to make the fourteen hour trek from Okinawa Japan to Washington and he died just an hour before we arrived. I'd been through death before but this was the first time with a parent. Though he was my husbands father, we had a good relationship and were as close as you can be with a military family of my own.

Up to now, most of my experiences with death were meaningful but not nearly so tragic for me. There were two friends, one died of cancer—the other of diabetes soon after. Then I insisted on being present when they put my dog to sleep. She lived till she was thirteen. For ten years now, I've kept her collar on my key chain as a memento. I had my own near death experience around the same time. Then last year my grandfather died. I didn't know him well but it got to me anyway. Still, none had carried the impact that Al's death did.

Physically, I totally lost the ability to control what was happening to me. My body was doing things I didn't give my permission to and it frightened me. For instance: I would reach up because I felt something on my cheek only to find I was crying and didn't know it. My legs shook for the first couple of days after he died and no amount of 'choice' would get them to stop. Mentally, I wasn't there at all. I would totally stop thinking and zone. It was like having a big blank spot in my mind that would wander. I couldn't remember anything. I would go hours without eating and think it was only a short time till my mother reminded me. Emotionally, I was numb. In short, everything I thought I knew went flying out the window. I couldn't affect what was going on at all.

Physician heal thyself. In my own innocence or perhaps arrogance, I thought I understood how trauma and grief worked but I didn't, not about this kind. In keeping with my own counsel—it was a chance to learn something when I could remember that's what I wanted to do. It was a truly humbling experience for me.

When I talked to my Mom about the whole thing, I was concerned about how this would affect my writing. My main thrust has been about choice and how you can use it to change things to become aware. But to learn that there are reactions that I can't control made me feel like a liar. One of my fears in writing this has been that the rape victim or someone whose house burned down killing their three children would read what I wrote about choice and say, 'Yeah right. She's never been through anything.' In fairness, I had but not like this. I'm happy to note I no longer serve that fear. Not because I think I know everything but because now I know I still have much to learn.

So what happened? I remember going back to my Mom and Dad's house after the funeral. I told my Mom I was going out to the hot tub. Took me a while to get there because I kept forgetting where I was going but I made it out there. I remember staring at the water and thinking briefly about choice. But no amount of attempted 'thinking' was working and I wondered if I were doomed to this forever. That's when a stray thought glanced me. Keep going. I remembered that I wrote that in some traumas, the urge is to stop everything to prevent further damage. So I made that my only thought when my brain was working. Keep going, don't stop. I held the thought for as long as I could each time it came up and the effort was, in itself, exhausting but it made all the difference in recovering from the shock. When I did have thoughts, they centered around continuance instead of how I could protect myself from what was happening and what I was feeling.

It's been a little over a month now as I write this and the experience has left me with a lot of questions, but it has gifted me with the understanding to write something that may help others. I wouldn't be so broad as to say that choice 'saved' me then. However, I did choose to stick with the thought 'keep going.' I literally willed myself to stay there as long as I could as often as I could.

I still assert, choose what you can. I guess that sometimes in life, choice becomes secondary, but it's still there and can be used to build your awareness even in the toughest of times. I took the opportunity to prove that to myself.

As I've commented before, This book was written over several years. I could simply exclude all the entries I've written while in the middle of lessons and give you the upshot, but I felt that the process is far more important than the outcome—so I've left them in. This section is especially poignant in that respect. It's now been four years since he's passed and so much has come of what I learned in those few days after he died. I've used my experience to help those I could deal with similar situations. I've also taken the experience and helped those preparing to die pass on with understanding and hopefully less fear. Were I to have wallowed in that initial pain causing that to grow—I have no doubt that the positive things that I've had the privilege to participate in since then would not have happened. You really never know, or could imagine in your wildest dreams, how something could turn out. You simply have to live it.

Conformity

This subject speaks directly to a fear society has of individual differences and how they use that fear against each other for the purposes of control and dominance. At some time in our lives, everyone experiences pressures that associate with this subject.

Let me first say that there are good conformities in that, they help to establish leadership and behavior that benefit the entire group. Then there are the bad ones that have the same characteristics but are applied against others. Oddly, even in these instances, when used carefully can promote good. For example: In the US, if there is a group of like-minded individuals who think that something the government is doing is wrong for whatever reason, they organize themselves and others around a single idea to change the status quo.

Now, before everyone gets stupid and starts burning their time cards thinking they have a right, let me jump on the conformity bandwagon for a moment. Employers have a right to expect their employees to be responsible. You have a right to go to lunch without worrying that someone will pull down their pants and dance on your table in an effort to prove they aren't conformists. Not all social expectations are negative.

How I think of it is in terms of the Golden Rule, the ultimate social rule in my opinion. What other rules do you need if you believe and follow this one? 'Do unto others as you would have them do unto you.' If you wouldn't like it, don't do it to someone else, a common respect for the lives and choices of others in exchange for your own rights. Simple. So simple that two thousand years after one of the arguably greatest teachers to grace the earth demonstrated how that rule could be lived, most people still don't get it. If they did, they would stop looking to blame the other guy/gal and learn to forgive, each other and themselves. What makes the Golden Rule so difficult to actually live instead of just believe in? For just one day, treat **everyone** as though they were someone you respected and cared personally for. Tell the truth, be kind and considerate. Then answer that question for yourself.

Conformity is easier. The rules are clear and responsibilities are few. Do as we say and you're in. You belong. Conformity thinks for you. This is right and this is wrong. Why? Because we say so and if you want to be with us, so do you. There is the thought that it would be easier to just live with whatever the particular rule is than to go against the whole to change the idea. After all, who wants all that rejection and judgment? Who would risk their 'place' to rock the boat?

Yet, our myths are full of such people. So while society sends the message, just live with it, be like us; all the stories we learn from teach us to think for ourselves. The character Luke Skywalker in Star Wars, who was expected to conform to the life his uncle had planned for him, longed for something else because he knew he wasn't who his uncle wanted him to be. There were several times in the story he could've just given up and conformed but he kept pushing, kept thinking, kept dreaming of more.

In Disney's *Beauty and The Beast*, Belle, unhappy with the 'provincial life' knew she wanted more. At any time she could've given in to public pressure, married the brutish hunter and lived the quiet life to please everyone else and gain acceptance. Instead she followed her dreams, even when she thought she'd given them up to save someone else. She never stopped living for herself. When faced with the wrath of the master of the castle or going to dinner with him to please him, she refused and honored herself.

Are these characters any different that the person standing at the water cooler? Perhaps you have dreams that you have allowed other to squash. Why did you not stand up for yourself and become what you wanted to be? It comes down to choice and awareness of self. These tools are used against the bane of conformity. These were characters who, despite confusion, frustration, and judgment rose to meet the challenge of the unknown and won their lives. It is the same lack of self awareness that causes the reaction of conformity.

Group Dynamics

'Wherever two or more of you are gathered…' there is a group. Wherever two or more are gathered there is the potential for fear and judgment, or love and acceptance. As humans, we have little choice in relation to involvement with the rest of the species. We are all on the same planet. If it can be said that Creator has a plan, then he or she stuck us all in the same room to play it out or destroy each other. The primary focus here is on freedoms and choice. Even the hermit on the mountain is affected in some way by the doings of his fellow Man and the choices of others. There is great fear in that and it shows most prominently within groups of individuals. Why? Bear with me; this gets complex.

The smoking debate is a wonderful example of how the fears of society handle choice. I am allergic to cigarette smoke. Not violently but I usually spend a painful few days recuperating after significant exposure. I tell 'smokers' (one group against the other) you have a choice to smoke or not. I don't have a choice. I must breathe if I want to live. My right comes before your choice. Now ask me how often they agree with me? Not often. And I don't get much understanding even when it's explained.

Consequently, I must limit my freedom based on anothers boundaries if I don't want to be sick all the time. This means waiting longer to get a nonsmoking table, moving if someone lights up next to me, forgoing some parties or club activities where smoking will be in an enclosed space, and suffering terribly during some overseas plane trips to name a few. What can I do? They have a right to choose smoking. This forces me to adapt instead of feeling free. The way I adapt is to differentiate myself from the 'smokers.' I judge them as insensitive idiots while I play the innocent party—the victim.

Now, ask yourself how you felt reading the last paragraph. Which group are you with, the smokers or nonsmokers? Are you a smoker but you don't fit the profile of an insensitive idiot? Then that's another group, the kinder, gentler smoker aware of the rights of others to the air. Always? Did you ask your kids if they mind second-hand smoke?

Are you a nonsmoker who doesn't agree with the labels I provided? Then you would take the side of a passive nonsmoker or whatever politically correct term you prefer. Or perhaps you're insensitive enough to not care one way or the other? My point is people, when challenged, quickly find allies for their point of view and justify it with judgment and fear.

Another example: There are few topics as hot group wise as the racial issues. Ask yourself this question: Is white skin different from black skin? Let us imagine that you answer yes. White is a different color than black. From the perspective of the light spectrum you are on the side of truth. It is a different color. Goody for you. How did this affect the whole? It didn't, except to discern between one thing and another. Discernment is a form of identification and orientation. Living in this reality, we must do that to find where we are and where we aren't.

Are white skinned people better than black skinned people? How you answer this determines a lot of things in relation to yourself and helps set the course for society as a whole. Yes, even just your one little answer affects the whole in some way because it colors your behavior and hides part of yourself from you in ways nothing else can.

Thoughts are energy that, in turn effect the energy of action. Here is where it begins, value judgment. This race is better or worse, this group is right or wrong, this person is nuts or sane, women are better than men. That I know I'm a woman doesn't limit me. Believing there is something too wrong or too right about it does. It affects how I treat others and how they will relate to me which affects society. Judgment assigns a personal or social value that limits the effectiveness of others. This limitation creates the fear and the need to fight back or protect.

On the other hand, I am not advocating wholesale elimination of judgment. In my experience that would be foolish. There is much to be learned by discovering your own judgments. I'm very much in favor of being aware of them for that reason alone.

I don't think it's realistic to expect the human animal to give up centuries of anger and defense in favor of peace and love. It would be great—but not realistic. But if, as an individual, you become aware of your judgments and learn to choose instead of reacting to them, and you teach someone else then perhaps over a time, fear will give over to love as a primary source of action. You must not work to eliminate a negative about yourself or anyone else. It makes the negative stronger when you fight it with fear. Work to understand it and assert your power of choice over it. That is courage. That's true love for yourself.

Group Mentalities

Great minds think alike. This is very true. Within the dynamic of the group, like minds feed or feed off of each other to gather energy and establish unity. Unity is essential to a group for this reason. Therefore, if you choose a specific group to devote your energy to like—Mothers Against Cookie Stealing Kids Wearing Bat Man Underwear or MAC-SKWBMU for short (got to have initials) you must conform your behavior to their mind set. The fear of individual or unique ideas within a group is a threat to unity which, in turn, threatens the mission objective—control. (How to keep Cody from the Keeblers)

The threat to mission objective (fear) is translated into 'We won't get what we want or they will.' Now we're beginning to sound like Creators spoiled little children. Any threat to the mission objective is interpreted on the individual and social level as failure. This completely invalidates the emotions and ideas of those associated with the group in question nullifying any power they may have. Now they have no respect, no understanding, and no Keeblers. So in order to validate your position, you gather with others and you pool energy toward accomplishing a single goal. What is really going on is the very same tug of war for energy that goes on in all communication. With a group, accumulated energy makes the prize much bigger—power over others.

Group Consciousness

Whenever two or more people gather their energy toward a single clear goal it creates tributaries of consciousness that becomes more than the sum of its parts. That's how love works miracles. When two people in love work together, no matter the differences between them, they serve the consciousness of the love they participate in. The 'relationship' becomes as a child between them to care for and nurture. It becomes its own entity, without body but with a will superior to the individual will of the participants.

When people gather with fear as a focus, they become servants to that fear. It's easy to tell when this happens because the fear of the whole will consume the individuals in the group. It creates an obsessive, addictive, dog-eat-dog mentality that strips all good intentions and feeds off of participants while still hungering for more. Fear oriented groups will offer little in return other than fear but will demand 110% from its members. Frequently they encourage if not demand that members bring others in.

How can you tell the difference between relationships and groups that center around love or fear? Watch how they fight. I'm not kidding! Love oriented groups or partners can disagree radically with each other and still come out of it whole. Fear oriented groups or couples eat each other alive with insults that wound personally, destroying anything good. Fear looks for blame and scapegoats. Love looks for cause, effect and solutions that benefit everyone involved. Fear gains in power by belittling and stealing personal power. Love strengthens, empowers, and heals its participants. In a sense, as we care for the consciousness of love, it cares for us as well. When it comes to the differences in love and fear, it's really absolute. How groups collectively participate in and react to these emotions becomes what we know as conformity. If it affects individual emotions and behavior, it is magnified when in groups.

The Individual Within the Group

The need to conform hits at the heart of many human motivations and fears—being alone. While you will find few people who will admit to it, the fear of being alone, in whatever sense your referring, is the sole motivating force to many of the modern day fears that have been identified.

Driven by this fear, people will do almost anything to be accepted by others. Some will create a fuss so they are the center of the attention. This is found in cases of criminal tendencies. Some will withdraw into themselves in hopelessness hoping someone will notice and come to rescue them. If someone responds to this mechanism, they will frequently find that they are ALWAYS rescuing that person and being consumed in the process. You find this in most cases of addiction.

Some become followers in order to fit in and conform to any wish of the whole that compels them. Some will appoint themselves leaders or others that want to be led will see the draw of attention and willingly follow whatever the request, rationalizing till it makes sense to them just to belong to something. Why?

Conformity, in and of itself, is merely a symptom of a much larger issue. I think we're struggling to be whole but have gotten that confused with having to belong to something or someone in order to be whole.

I would be the first to agree that it is a myopic view. I believe that because I have never felt whole. I've been forever looking for the place to belong and be accepted. To do that I needed to fit in. In your heart of hearts, reading this now can you say you ever felt whole? No one I've talked or worked with can. I believe everyone experiences the sensation or feeling that something is missing in life, but they just don't know what it is. So, like me, they look for something to fill the space never knowing that what's missing is themselves.

All these things we've discussed in Chapter Four, are the attitudes and dispositions that people grow up with and make themselves into. They hold as much illusion as they do truth. How many identities do you have right now? Mother—Father—Supervisor—Patient... How many stereotypes are you forced to deal with every day? Woman—Man—Teenager—Racial Persuasion—Lawyer... None of these are who you are. But by knowing how to find them and putting them in their proper place, you gain the freedom to see what is there. Who you really are—not what you've been told or what you believe must be true.

Love

There are those who feel that Creator is missing in our lives, not ourselves. I too thought that for a time until I realized that, if creation is peeking out from every atom then the problem must be that we do not see it. My inquisitive mind screamed for an explanation. Why can we not see if it's always there? Something fundamental in our relationship with Creator was missing. The kicker is that for everyone the mechanism is different since we are all different. The irony is that every path leads to the same thing but we must get there in our own way. "Many paths, one journey."

I knew then that any 'finding' of Creator I did wasn't going to mean anything if I wasn't willing to receive it. To me, it didn't make much difference that Creator loved me when I was wallowing in my own insecurities. I couldn't share that love; I couldn't experience it. I wasn't worth it. And so began my first step. The oppressive emotion of realizing that I truly thought I wasn't worth any kind of love was devastating but it explained a lot.

When I thought deeply about it, I wasn't even sure I knew what love really was. My parents loved me, that I know. But what did that mean? My friends loved me but what did it mean? Was I responsible for that? What was it that they loved? I was riddled with these agonizing questions. And at the top of the list, why did Creator love me? That's something I've been both blessed and cursed with knowing. There were times in my life that I questioned the nature of Creator but never what I felt from that source. I definitely didn't feel worth it but I desperately needed it.

It wasn't till I had my own children that some of these questions began to settle into some kind of recognizable picture. The first time I looked into my child's eyes I knew what love was even if I couldn't define it. I also knew that it was that form of love that was missing in my life. That love was me. I sat in judgment of myself in regard to worth. I prevented myself from participating in the experience of love. And with a child now who was going to need the whole instead of the part, I could no longer afford the luxury of self pity and recrimination. I didn't want him to learn to hate himself from me.

First thing I learned; real love hurts. Unconditional love hurts more. But as my mother would say, it's a good hurt. I called it growing pains of the soul, expanding so it could accommodate more instead of less. I'd been so filled up with less that to have any at all was extremely painful. I think that's why most people never pursue a path of unconditional love. It's not the blissful rainbow filled experience it's reported to be at first.

The strength of the flow as it returns is daunting and does take some getting used to. Your choices change because the protective voice isn't gunking up the flow anymore. In some ways, you feel vulnerable because that protective layer of fear is gone. But in its place is something that cannot be manipulated or taken away because it's yours and only you know how and why it works for you.

Healing is a warrior art. When you truly heal something, it cannot be used against you. In a very real way, you have to earn it to own it. No weapon is stronger than that which you are.

I have not yet resolved the question of evil for myself. But I do know if there is an evil intelligence, it doesn't control us. It has no power other than the good bits of ourselves we willingly give up to fear and judgment. Understand those and you become difficult to abuse. Know yourself and no matter what happens to you, what oddity or unexpected thing happens in your life here, inside you will be free. I know for myself, that makes all the difference. Know yourself and you know others. Know yourself and you know Creator. I can't prove that and don't really have a mind to, for those wondering. I can and only do speak from my own experience. Now for me, conformity is a matter of choice.

Everyone sometime in their lives has known what it meant to love. Not the kind that is so casually tossed around in the English language, "I love this table!" The kind of love that comes with all the anticipation, depth, hope and delicious confusion that only it can. It's the kind of love that recognizes that not only are we not alone in this world but that we are only but a part of a living web that recreates life every second of the day, every breath we take.

I heard it described once in a way that was truth to me. "I love as trees love the sun, as grass loves green." Whether the direction of the love is a person or Creator, the essence of the emotion distilled is the same subject. In love of any kind, you know you aren't alone. That's why fear is the opposite of love. Fear must be alone. Love can be part of the whole without diminishing itself in the process.

Exercise

Just for a moment, let go and allow yourself to enjoy the experience of LOVE itself—as if it were it's own consciousness. It really is an extraordinary sensation that has a way of changing your views entirely. When I did this I looked at it this way, "What did I have to lose?" I was entirely skeptical for several reasons. First, you had to have something or someone to love—a direction, if you will, for the flow. I didn't have that so I couldn't. 'Creators' love wasn't what I was after at the time.

I wanted something more tangible and provable to me at the time. I still had so many questions about the divine nature of life that questions got in the way of the experience. Then I got this seemingly bizarre idea to me. What if… Over the centuries love has been attributed to many things. Chemical reactions, Gods and goddess blessings, fate and others. What if…, like a cold will pass from person to person, love also does? I'd seen negative emotions do that. They spread like a wildfire. Why couldn't love?

People can accomplish the impossible whenever love is present. Then the scary thought followed. What if love is always present, we just don't know it? So with all that reasoning and questioning, I formed a thought I could use. Was love a sentient energy—a consciousness apart from what we think of as a host? Just as light passes in and around us, does love?

With this thought, I began to meditate. I was on a hunt. I have no way to prove this beyond my own experience so you'll just have to judge for yourself and your own experience, which is strangely appropriate I think. But like I told my fears, "What have I got to lose but you?" A funny thing about fears—they were more afraid then I was.

Step One—Get comfortable in a place you'll be undisturbed. Have some music you know well going at the time and feel like getting into. Whether it's Vavaldi, Yanni, or Twisted Sister, doesn't matter so long as you can get into it.

Step Two—Preparation: Focus on the music, breathing slowly and deliberately in and out. Listen for the main melody line. In your mind—isolate the theme hearing all else as the background. Allow yourself to feel the theme, deep in your heart. Draw it in. Feel it resonate and echo in all of the cells of your body and spirit. I can't tell you how you'll feel it. I can just tell you that you know it when it happens. You become the flow of the song, without expectation or intention. When you feel this stage, move on to step three.

Step Three—Gently shift your attention to the rhythm of the song. This is accomplished with the same ease as simply shifting your gaze to see another object. Become aware that this beat was there all the time you were focusing on the theme. Allow yourself to purposely draw in the rhythm with each breath, becoming deeply aware of it thrumming in your body and the air around you. Feel the sound reach from the air around you through your muscles and to your bones. Atoms inside and outside you become infused with the presence of song.

Step Four—Shift your attention to a harmony in the song. Become aware that this was there all the time, supporting the body of the music with quiet satisfaction. Draw it fully into your awareness, breathing it in a till it becomes a part of the whole awareness you've built, all parts of the music moving together blended into song. It's in the space around you; it moves the force of life within and without your physical form.

Hold this thought: the harmony in our song of life is experienced as love. Allow your soul to be aware of its essence. This is who and what you really are. Savor the sensation of love for it's own sake. Drink it in.

Step Five—Allow yourself to let that love go. It is not something to hold on to for if you do, you'll stop the flow and become fearful. Then sense its return. Receive, return, receive, return…each time it flows it grows, with each breath, with each thought. Love cannot exist in a vacuum of anxious one-sided thoughts. Only in a flow.

Step Six—When you're ready to end the exercise, gradually return your attention back to just your body and where you are here and now.

Please, take your time adjusting your attention. When I did this, I jumped up, I was so excited. Then fell right back down on my butt. Nothing was injured but my pride. This is not something to be taken lightly or casually.

Last Words

If at first you don't succeed at this, do it till you do. It's not something that generally happens overnight unless you've been ready for it for a long time. In order to be effective in your own healing, you must be in touch with this core-self because this is where you begin. Identity/illusions created by years of conditioning and learned behavior has taught you that core-self must be protected or hidden from everyone—including yourself. I'm not saying to do away with identities. I'm saying they aren't the core of who and what you really are but rather secondary reflections of what's acceptable. You can't cure the disease by playing around with just the symptoms. You have to go to the root of the malady. In this case, the disease is illusion—the cure is truth. Once found, you know the way back.

By tuning to your core-self, the insecurities of rejection and judgment have no hold on you. From that moment on, no one can tell you who you are because you will know. You begin to make effective choices for yourself based on who you are rather than who you aren't. And life becomes something to enjoy not endure.

Journal Space

Chapter Five

Creating Space

First Words

In this chapter we'll explore the gifts of nothingness and learn how to create them for yourself. There are a few exercises in this chapter instead of just one.

Material Preparation:	Earplugs
	Notes from Chapters One and Four

The Gifts of Nothingness

Do you ever catch yourself saying that you have no time...no energy ...then the first thing you need to learn is to create space? Imagine a crowded room; every inch of floor space is covered with stuff. Then imagine stuff on top of that stuff so that vertical space is practically useless. That is your internal mind, filled with the stuff of your life; crammed with McDonalds commercials, deadlines, preferences, fights, worries...just about anything you can think of or intend to think of soon. Like a miser, you horde everything that you think you need to survive in this world and you keep it in such an inefficient space when all you really need is more room.

Conventional and logical thought suggests that if you want to make space, you must do away with things. Space is finite. You want room in your closet, toss a bunch of stuff you don't need anymore out. Creating space internally is something different and not as threatening to your inner mind set. It's more like seeing the space that's already there.

In the tiny little world of atoms, protons and electrons circle a nucleus, in its simplest explanation. To enable movement—there must be a space in which to be. In fact—from what scientists know now, there's more space then mass. So follow this—for every atom, and there are lots, there is space around and within them or there would be no movement. Consider the words you're reading. They are organized ink stains pinned onto a white space with far more space than ink. Would they be as legible if not for the space between? As understandable?

So lets take a closer look at the function of space in our lives. I happen to love thesauruses for getting to the root of what a word really means in our conceptual thought. You can use the word space—simple, or you can expand the concept by choosing the word void. Gives it a cooler more spacious feeling. If you want a deeper sense to it—use abyss. If you wanted a more epoch feeling, the word oblivion adds the element of time to the concept. If you're going for that hopeless feeling—emptiness works. But for the simplest conceptual idea for space,

I'd have to say that space is what exists in between what we recognize as material reality. What exists between heartbeats? What dwells between the notes of a song? What keeps the atoms of a cell from crashing into each other? What is in between our thoughts? If they move, if there's a flow of energy, there must be a space for them to move in? What does space have to do with our growth?

In Tao, it is said that the space is what makes a thing useful. For instance, a cup wouldn't be useful as a cup without the space in the center. A wheel wouldn't be able to fulfill its purpose without a center from which to rotate. So in a very real sense, all that *is* relies on all that *isn't* to lend shape it's purpose. As I said in Chapter One, every soul needs somewhere to be. So far we've concerned ourselves with what is. Now, lets turn our attention to what isn't.

Your life is full of holes! Look around you with an eye for space. The shell of your TV set has a hole. Bookshelves have space for books. Drawers have space for storage. Closets, pots and pans, toilets, holes are everywhere, even in your own body. If space is that important to the existence and movement of matter—how much more important is it in spiritual development. And yet, it's something easily overlooked as it is always there where matter isn't and it can be very difficult to define.

They are mutually defining—what is and what isn't. Kinda like opposites define each other by virtue of their existence. We know what's true by what's false and verse visa. We know what's in by what's out and verse visa. We know what isn't by what is and verse visa.

What does space mean to your internal dynamics? Simply put, what is there to learn when all the room is taken? It gives the illusion that all has been learned and nothing more is needed. You're filled up to capacity. If you did that to your physical environment, how would you navigate your home? There would be too much stuff. No movement would be possible. So as important as skills, learning and experience is to your growth, development, and healing, so is creating and maintaining space. Let's examine some trouble-free ways to create space in your life.

Listening

Learn to listen. This is the art of being receptive in communication and what I believe to be a critical step in spiritual development. If your mind is busy with stuff you think you know, your positive about, should believe but doubt, want to believe but are afraid to, need to do, have to do, want to have...how can you hear yourself think? If you can't hear yourself think, how can you 'listen' the words of others? How many times have you sat outside and not heard the birds chirping? How many times have you really listened to them and what they have to say?

A busy mind has no time to conceive anything outside itself. A mind that is absolutely positive about what it knows has no room for growth or imagination (and no time for bird song). You are certain that this book is solid—but is it really or does it just appear to be? Those are two different realities. One offers a peek at freedom, the other the comfort of a resolved reality. If atoms are constantly in motion—nothing is solid as we understand the idea. Think about it. The molecules of the words on this page are in motion! Is that extraordinary to contemplate? How are you really interacting with that energy exchange?

When you talk with a friend, do you listen or just hear? Hearing is a mechanical process where, in simplest terms, sound waves travel through the atmosphere—some of it passing your tympanic membrane. It excites the nervous system making your eardrum move. These impulses trigger more bio-electrical energy that goes from the cochlea to the brain where it's interpreted as the sound of a metal pot falling to the ground. Your friend talks to you and the same mechanical process happens.

Real listening means that, rather than the passive mechanics of sound physiology, you accept what is said to you on the emotional and mental levels of communication. It is a receptive state, free of judgement. Your mind is quiet—no distractions, no doubts, no fears that interfere with what you're receiving. How do you do that? You create a space by learning to listen to yourself, in a literal sense.

Exercise

Obtain a pair of earplugs and put them in your ears. **Only do this if it is safe for you to do so.** Sit in stillness for a moment and listen to your body. Focus until you can hear your heart beating. Image that…the sound of your living body. It's an amazing thought to me that I'm seldom aware of it in there pumping away with every breath I take. Like the sound of your footsteps or the rhythm of a drum, it beats, steady and strong. Focus deeply and imagine you can hear what it's telling you as if it were words or perhaps a song. Write about that.

Now as incredible an experience as that may be, and for me it is every time, that is still the study of matter and substance, not space. So now, focus again on your heartbeat but as you increase your focus—zoom in on the space between the beats. As you zoom in and magnify your vision of that space, it becomes larger. Thought falls away—even your command of focus on the space will dissolve into the being of it as you become more practiced.

This is what creating space is about and once you experience it—you realize that everything is everything and it has its importance to be sure. But the 'nothing' is where your being truly is. In finding your Connection to Creator, the connection is important as the study of a something. But the nothing is where Creator is complete. Everything springs from the nothingness and to the nothingness it returns.

As you gradually direct your focus back to the beat, add your new focus of the space to your awareness of this world. Next time your friend is talking to you, remember where you found space within and be there again.

The idea is not to fill the space up with identity or listening as such, but rather to create an emptiness to use as a balance in your life. When you begin to feel crowded, misunderstood, persecuted or just plain trodden on, increase your awareness of the nothingness within everything to create space between you and whatever it is troubling. This has a balancing effect that will enable you to use a new perspective and see other possible outcomes to situations you may not have been able to think of within the deluge of everything.

Something With Nothing

One aspect of nothingness is that it actively shapes the reality around you. Lets say you want a table to go in the corner of your diningroom. You take out a tape measure and figure out how broad a table can comfortably fit into the space available and happily go shopping. Finally, after searching high and low—you find the table of your dreams. Pulling out your tape measure, you discover to your disappointment that the table is too large to fit in the space you've decided to put it in. You'll have to find a more suitable table and off you go.

Space has just defined your reality. It happens all the time. What's the big deal about that? If space/nothingness is constantly defining your reality but your attention is always on the material something, it can affect balance internally. The same situation as above will find the internal dynamics happening something like this; 'I can't have what I want. I can't have what I choose.' It's an attempt by your personality to interpret the material limitations you perceive into something understandable so you can act on it accordingly. In a situation like this though, you've given yourself nothing to act on and that thinking loop creates pressure.

The challenging thing is to learn to interpret through choice instead and this is accomplished by being able to see other possibilities. Seeing other possibilities is accomplished by adding the infinite to perceived limitations. When you do that you find that you could add on to the room, though you may not want to. That's a choice. You could rearrange the room so it would accommodate what you want, another choice… Knowing you do have choices, that, in reality it isn't limited in the ways you thought, internally relieves the pressure caused by false boundaries. Then it balances out.

Big deal—no one can have everything they want? Let's expand this scenario and watch the ripple effect. You can't have the one you fell in love with so you shop and find one that will fit. It's not what you wanted but it'll work. You trudge home with it. Already the ripples are beginning to affect your reality. You arrange it in its place and think about how often you are going to have to stare at it. It's not bad. It's just not what you wanted. Every day—you will have that thought, maybe more than once a day. That energy is sneaking up on you.

A friend comes over and has a reaction to the table you found. Whether good or bad, the story will come out about how you didn't get what you wanted. Why? The energy remains unbalanced and unresolved. So you have to go over it and over it in an attempt to finish it once and for all. Let's assume someone hates it and then you must defend a choice you didn't want to make in the first place. Up it comes again building on a negative foundation until it transforms inside you into a concrete reality. Now you hate that table, you argue with everyone who says anything about it and you fantasize about what a lovely expensive fire it would make if only you'd bought the house with a fireplace. Course if you'd bought that house—you would have had a bigger diningroom. The little things DO matter.

Potential

In the writing of this book I've spent many a day staring at a blank screen, or in the days before I got a computer, a blank page. It took some staring before I saw something that had eluded me. The blank page that had become my accuser, judge, jury and taskmaster wasn't empty at all. It was full of potential. It could be anything or nothing at all. It could be a colorful origami swan among a thousand flying on a wing and a wish of some child far away. It could be a canvas for an epic poem passed from generation to generation, finally finding immortality through written verse. It could be the half-baked note of a serial killer used as conclusive evidence against him. It could be the springboard for glowing characters in the next popular novel. Wadded up, it's an instant cat toy. It could be the first written words of some ancient Babylonian text long forgotten to time—or simply a page of words you are interacting with now.

Potential is a future aspect of nothingness. It is the birthplace of imagination and inspiration, where disjointed ideas coalesce to form innovative concepts; where what is capable of being finds balance in reality. With it, we've been to the moon and back. We dream paths to other universes, other realities or reach deep inside of ourselves to explore the secrets of creation.

I get up and work every day because of what could be, not in the future but in every moment. There is a passion for me that comes with this form of expression. I am no longer who I think I am or who I'm afraid I may be—I enter a space within of neutrality where those things don't influence my actions. It transforms me from the 'little me' (limited by thoughts, habits, and routines) into the larger experience of possibility. In a sense, I forget myself to the experience because I live within the potential of the moment.

How many of you ponder your potential at all? How many of you have just accepted that life is the way it is for you and always will be? Believe, if even for a moment that you could *BE* more. Believe for the barest twinkling that you *ARE* more. Why not? It's so easy to believe you are less. Why would it be so tough to turn that around if only for a second and feel your potential—allow room for possibilities? Think hard—it's important…

Yet the majority of people would rather believe the worst about themselves and limit their power—limit their space within to the dreary confines of social and habitual ballast. What potential are you giving up to keep what you don't even want? That is where your power is dissipating.

Exercise

What do you do to turn it around? Go back to the lists you made in Chapters One and Four. Outline where you recognize that you are limiting potential in your life and name the limitations. Then add the infinite of potential. This section of growth is more ambiguous than and exact science but in the adding of the infinite to your perceived limitations, you'll be able to conquer any roadblocks you may come up against as you travel your journey. It's such a simple equation really. Limitation + space = transformation.

Nothingness as a Mirror

Nothingness is just that. In being that, it's the only thing with the capacity to accurately reflect the material world. Two mirrors directly across from each other, with an object between them will reflect the exact same thing. This is a matter to matter reflection—a finite. A mirror reflects a chair—matter to matter interaction. Water reflects your face—matter to matter interaction. Only what is substantial can be reflected back to you. Because of this property—it will have a tendency to bounce back and forth as your mind struggles to find differences. It is critical in thoughts and decision making to discern differences but, in this direct reflection process, it will go over and over the same old thing. The mind closes in on only those thoughts and, seeing no differences, the thought becomes trapped within the dueling reflections. This process creates pressure, becoming worry, fear, tension, distraction, brooding, struggle, anxiety, etc.

When you use nothingness as a force of reflection, the material world becomes an infinite reflection while the nothingness remains nothingness. Here, your mind will recognize differences and expand. The mind opens to the emptiness and finds infinity—transforming what was finite into an infinite. In the mirror of our thoughts and minds, it is a fine line to draw but an important one to spiritual growth. Without infinite vision, the feeling and experience that there is something beyond the pain, the anger, the heartache—negativity becomes your master instead of your teacher and balance point. Transformation becomes almost impossible under these conditions.

Exercise

How Do You Use It?

You cannot 'think' nothing because then you're thinking something. It's weird that way. So in a meditation it isn't effective to think—'I'm thinking nothing' ...You must learn to *BE* nothing. As simple as that—but not easy.

To be nothing is to cultivate a **state of being what isn't**, including identity. If you think, 'I'm being nothing'—that won't lead you there either because of the reference to your identity. It's a state of being that is completely in the moment but, if you think—'I'm being in the moment' then that moment will pass before you finish the thought and you'll be behind the state of being.

The difference between western meditations and eastern ones, as I see it, is that eastern meditations cultivate the states of being. In the westernized versions, meditations are used as behavior modification and self-examination. Those are very busy meditations involving Chi breathing, identity perceptions (I'm this or that), repetition of a theme (smoking, weight loss, etc.), and focus on relaxation (which preoccupies the mind with the struggle to achieve a goal). Eastern meditations are geared toward achieving a balanced state of being. This is involves acceptance of struggle, not an ongoing fight to achieve dominance over it. In doing so, you go past the illusion of struggle to see what's really going on. Once there, you can make an effective choice. Once a choice is made, the energy is free. Once your life becomes more about choice than struggle, you can begin on the state of being.

I began with the listening method at the beginning of this chapter. I'd turn my attention to the space between heartbeats and hold it there as long as I could. If thoughts came up, I literally turned away from them and to that space. When I could achieve that for a good length of time, I willed myself to move into the space. This is where I found the experience of being nothing.

Last Words

Here's where it gets tough to describe.

Since the nothingness is nothing, when you're truly within it, 'you' aren't. I noticed that as I moved closer to perceived proximity, my thoughts slowed to nothing. It was as if they could find nothing to work with, no energy, and nothing to receive them so they slowed to a stop and then there really was *nothing*. My sense of 'me' dissolved and expanded at the same time. It felt like entering an ocean. There is a sense of massiveness and weight to the experience, not physically but spiritually—as if you entered the universe at the same time it entered you. When in this state, everything you are is mirrored by everything you aren't. This state is, in itself transformative. The more practiced you become in achieving this state, the more it becomes a part of your life and perception.

Journal Space

Afterword

Now begins the real work and you have the rest of your life to live and practice the truths you've found through this book. My goal was to craft in such a way that, no matter where you are on your path, there will always be something of value to be found no matter how many times you read it.

There's so much more beyond these lessons and truths; one thing always leads to another. Don't stop here with my words. As I said in the beginning of the book, this is all my experience and I share it in hopes that you'll find or create your own to share and help someone else reach farther. I'd like to leave you with a few thoughts…

1. This path has been trod by others but is far from worn. The path may be the same but we all have our own unique way of walking it. Take care with your steps.

2. Seek out the areas of your life where you've become a servant to fear or confusion, and heal them with what you have learned.

3. Begin to validate yourself and you will not need anyone else to do it for you.

4. When you feel lost—go to the beginning to find your way.

5. When you feel alone—remember that in a world of more than three billion people plus animals and plants, you're never technically alone.

6. When you use the word 'everyone'- include yourself. It offers valuable insights into what you're thinking and feeling.

7. Remember that nothing lasts forever—there is always change. (How long is forever anyway?)

8. Remember that nothing real can be threatened.
9. Define value and then live it.

An American Indian blessing: Walk in beauty and balance. (In all things strive for balance.)

And above all, 'To thine own self, be true.'

Wishing you well on your journey,

Silver Eagle

About the Author

Silver Eagle is a mother of two, wife of 16 years, healer, musician, writer, artist, Taekwondo black belt, housekeeper, and minister. She's often found cuddling with her kitty or wrapping her brain around physics. Other interests include comparative religion and physiology.

Appendix

In A Rut?

Here are just a few easy and fun ways to coax a bit of change into your life without disrupting the current flow. Sometimes, simply entering into a new experience transforms how you see yourself and the world around you. With a bit of effort—you CAN transform your life!

1. Learn a new language. You don't have to sign up for a class or do anything complicated. Just go to your library and see what's available in tapes, computer programs or books and work at your own pace. Soon you could be speaking Spanish, German, French, Greek, etc. Who knows? If you become fluent, apply for jobs that require translator and embark on a new career. Get a friend to learn with you and change your life together! If you spend two hours in the car coming home from work, perfect time to listen to a language tape.

2. Practice a martial art. There are martial arts for all ages and capabilities. You can find tapes and books all over the place if you're the self teaching type. Join a class and, for a few hours a week you get to kick your troubles away. Great for stress and focus.

3. Start a hobby. You want the kid of activity that, while you're engaged in the activity, you lose track of time. Course then you'll need a timer of some kind as well. Some hobbies take only the time you can give. Others are a bit more demanding. You never know when a hobby can turn into something for a lifetime. Need a unique gift for the holidays or just someone special? Make it yourself! Here are a few ideas to get you thinking:

Origami—the Japanese Art of Paper Folding , Fossil Hunting, Cooking, Gardening, Knitting/Crochet , Wood Working, Wood Burning, Quilt, Stained Glass, Gem Faceting, Bee keeping, Gourd Crafting, Beading, Candle, soap, and oil making, Framing, Painting, Bird Watching, Photography, Movie Making, Writing, Rubber Stamping, Paper Making, Magic Tricks, Juggling, Leather Work

4. Learn to play an instrument. Even if you are tone deaf, you can still learn to play and instrument. I've played violin since 6th grade and expanded my abilities into viola, keyboard and drums. You don't have to be a virtuoso—it just has to make you happy and who knows where it will lead?

5. Volunteer for something. For some, volunteer is a nasty word. It means sacrifice and usually no fun. But there are many ways to volunteer a bit of yourself and have fun too.

Talk to your local hospital about bone marrow and blood drives. You can set them up for where you work, at your local mall, at a church, at a hall… You just might save a life. Have organ donor cards available for people who want them and save a few more.

Talk to your library about reading to kids.

Go to a local nursing home and give some time to the elderly.

Deliver flowers at a hospital or talk to them about volunteer positions.

If you have a spare $20 bucks—buy a bunch of flowers and hand them out to just anyone. You never know whose day you'll brighten and you'll feel pretty good too.

Scouts are always looking for volunteers.

6. Collect something. Just about everything can be collected. Sometimes it's nice to see the fruits of your labors. It doesn't have to be anything elaborate. I've collected drinking straws before just cause they made me smile. (Ok, that's a little weird but you get the idea) Don't turn it into a competition with the neighbors. Just participate in something you can look forward to that makes you smile.

7. Once a day, do something you wouldn't ordinarily do for someone else—whether they appreciate it or not. The idea is to reach outside yourself without expectation of return and see what happens. Open the door for that guy at the office you hate. Fill a cup of coffee for the person that ticked you off the day before. Wave to all the babies you can. It's corney but fun!

8. Get a pet. Again, doesn't have to be anything complicated. I had a friend who had tarantulas. I have a kitty whose convinced she's human. A pet probably won't 'change your life' but they can enrich it.

9. And the number one easiest way to change your life—**laugh** because hey, it's funny. Nothing really makes sense…

Suggested Reading

These are a few books I keep around in my own library. They've been my guidance, resource material and companions for many years. In no particular order:

The Tao of Being—Ray Grigg

Earth Medicine—Jamie Sams

Power of Myth—Joseph Campbell

The Warrior is Silent—Scott Shaw Ph.D

The Four Fold Way—Angeles Arrien Ph.D

The Path to Power—SunBear, Wabun Wind, Berry Weinstock

365 Day Tao—Deng Ming-Dao

Groliers Multimedia Encyclopedia

Random House Websters Dictionary

Holes and Other Superficialities—Roberto Casati and Achille C Varzi

The God Particle—Leon Lederman with Dick Teresi

Ki In Daily Life—Koichi Tohei

The Physiology Coloring Book—Wynn Kapit/ Robert I Macey/ Esmail Meisami

Don't Know Much About the Bible—Kenneth C. Davis

The Tao of Gung Fu—Bruce Lee